Hello. If I have been silly enough to
mislay this diary please return it to:
Mr. Bean
c/o Mrs. Wicket
"Daffodils"
12 Arbor Road
LONDON N10
A £5-00 reward would certainly not be
out of the question.

Library of Congress Catalog Card Number: 94-72372

First published in the UK in 1993 by
Boxtree Limited,
Broadwall House,
21 Broadwall,
London SE1 9PL

Designed by Nigel Davies for Titan Studio.
Photography by Paul Forrester.

Front cover photograph of Mr. Bean courtesy of Stephen F. Morley.
Back cover photograph of Mr. Bean courtesy of Thames Television.

HIGHBURY DISTRICT COUNCIL DIARY

Compiled by Robin Driscoll and Rowan Atkinson

Andrews and McMeel
A Universal Press Syndicate Company
Kansas City

HIGHBURY DISTRICT COUNCIL

LIGHT SWITCH

BED

SHUT UP!

Mayor
Sarah Mahaffy
32 Tongdean Rise,
London N5

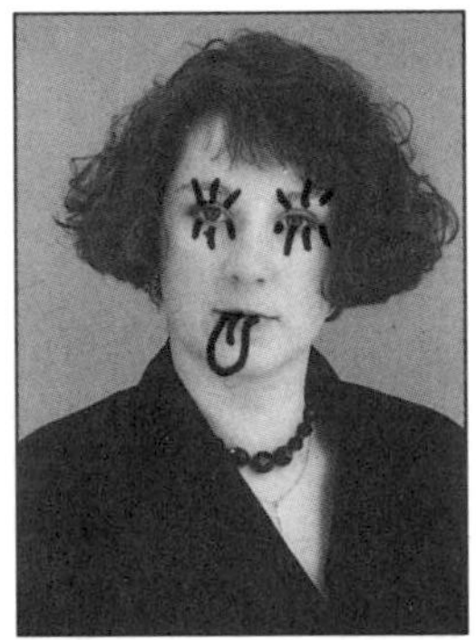

Councillor
Nichola Motley
Housing Committee
Broadwaters,
308 Waldergrave Rd,
London N5

Councillor David Inman
Planning Committee
29 Duchland Avenue, London NW8

Councillor Susan Cole
Environment Committee
Flat 3, 21 Downlands Close, London N9

Councillor Chantel Noel
Women's Committee
c/o Highbury Town Hall

Councillor Rod Green
Policy Committee
c/o Highbury Town Hall

Councillor Adrian Sington
Emergency Committee
Church Villas, 15 Dukes Road, London N5

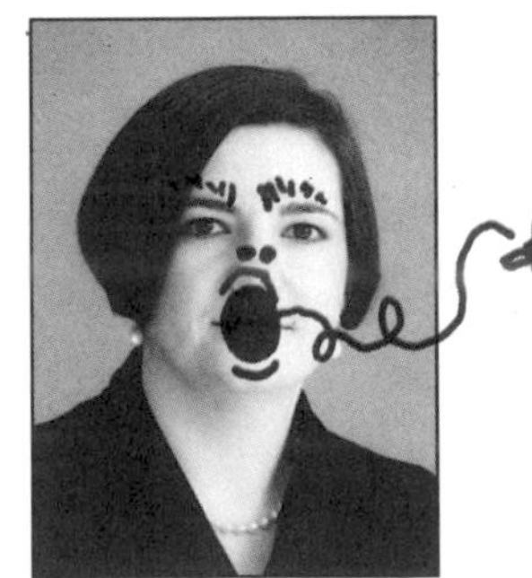

Councillor Elaine Collins
Equal Oportunities Committee
4a George Street, London NW4

Temperature Conversions

°C	°F	°C	°F	°C	°F	°C	°F	°C	°F	°C	°F
-20	-4.0	1	33.8	22	71.6	43	109.4	64	147.2	85	185.0
-19	-2.2	2	35.6	23	73.4	44	111.2	65	149.0	86	186.8
-18	-0.4	3	37.4	24	75.2	45	113.0	66	150.8	87	188.6
-17	1.4	4	39.2	25	77.0	46	114.8	67	152.6	88	190.4
-16	3.2	5	41.0	26	78.8	47	116.6	68	154.4	89	192.2
-15	5.0	6	42.8	27	80.6	48	118.4	69	156.2	90	194.0
-14	6.8	7	44.6	28	82.4	49	120.2	70	158.0	91	195.8
-13	8.6	8	46.4	29	84.2	50	122.0	71	159.8	92	197.6
-12	10.4	9	48.2	30	86.0	51	123.8	72	161.6	93	199.4
-11	12.2	10	50.0	31	87.8	52	125.6	73	163.4	94	201.2
-10	14.0	11	51.8	32	89.6	53	127.4	74	165.2	95	203.0
-9	15.8	12	53.6	33	91.4	54	129.2	75	167.0	96	204.8
-8	17.6	13	55.4	34	93.2	55	131.0	76	168.8	97	206.6
-7	19.4	14	57.2	35	95.0	56	132.8	77	170.6	98	208.4
-6	21.2	15	59.0	36	96.8	57	134.6	78	172.4	99	210.2
-5	23.0	16	60.8	37	98.6	58	136.4	79	174.2	100	212.0
-4	24.8	17	62.6	38	100.4	59	138.2	80	176.0	101	213.8
-3	26.6	18	64.4	39	102.2	60	140.0	81	177.8	102	215.6
-2	28.4	19	66.2	40	104.0	61	141.8	82	179.6	103	217.4
-1	30.2	20	68.0	41	105.8	62	143.6	83	181.4	104	219.2
0	32.0	21	69.8	42	107.6	63	145.4	84	183.2	105	221.0

Conversion Values

Distance

miles to kilometres	1.6093
yards to metres	0.9144
feet to metres	0.3048
inches to millimetres	25.4
inches to centimetres	2.54

Area

square miles to square kilometres	2.59
square miles to hectares	258.99
acres to square metres	4046.86
acres to hectares	0.4047
square yards to square metres	0.8361
square feet to square metres	0.0929
square feet to square centimetres	929.03
square inches to square centimetres	645.16
square inches to square millimetres	6.4516

Volume

cubic yards to cubic metres	0.7646
cubic feet to cubic metres	0.0283
cubic inches to cubic centimetres	16.3871

Capacity

gallons to litres	4.546
quarts to litres	1.137
pints to litres	0.568
gills to litres	0.142

Speed

miles per hour to kilometres per hour	1.6093
feet per second to metres per second	0.3048
feet per minute to metres per second	0.0051
feet per minute to metres per minute	0.3048
inches per second to millimetres per second	25.4
inches per minute to millimetres per second	0.4233
inches per minute to millimetres per minute	2.54

Mass → 10.00 St. Marys

tons to kilograms	1016.05
tons to tonnes	1.0160
hundredweights to kilograms	50.8023
centals to kilograms	45.3592
quarters to kilograms	12.7006
stones to kilograms	6.3503
pounds to kilograms	0.4536
ounces to grams	28.3495

HEEHEEHEEHEE

Mass per Unit Area STUPID

tons per square mile to kilograms per square hectare	3.923
pounds per sq. foot to kilograms per sq. metre	4.8824
pounds per sq. inch to grams per sq. centimetre	70.307
ounces per sq. foot to grams per sq. metre	305.152

Mass per Unit Length

tons per mile to kilograms per metre	0.6313
pounds per foot to kilograms per metre	1.4882
pounds per inch to kilograms per metre	17.858
ounces per inch to grams per millimetre	1.1161

Fuel Consumption

gallons per mile to litres per mile	2.825
miles per gallon to kilometres per litre	0.354

Addresses & Telephone Numbers

The Queen
Buckingham Palace (Flat No.?)
London
ENGLAND

Ex directory

Inspector Morse
Oxford Nick
Oxfordshire

999

~~Linda Gobb~~
~~Highbury Library~~
~~Highbury~~

Prime Minister
10 Downing Street
London (Weekdays)

071 290 3000

Chequers (W/ends)

0945 482451
(PayPhone — Pub)

Shirley Bassey
On my Wall
In my room
My House
My Street
ENGLAND

081 467 8290

~~Mr. Wilkinson~~

KILL KILL
KILL

Addresses & Telephone Numbers

GOD
Everywhere (literally, apparently)

Crematorium
(That place in the trees with the chimney) 081 858 5010

Mum
Clapham Cemetery

Grandad
~~[illegible] Grove Road~~
~~LONDON NW[illegible]~~
(Moved in with Mum) → Shroud Store 071 736 5926

December

25 Friday Christmas Day

Oooh! Diary for Christmas

Xmas '92

3pm Queen

26 Saturday

Boxing Day?

27 Sunday

??

Still no sign of Boxing Day

December

28 Monday Boxing Day

~~Dear Mrs. Queen~~ 11:00 Corner Shop
~~Dear Eliz~~ PILCHARDS

Dear The Queen

I hope you are well. I am fine. A most peculiar thing has happened. You may remember that last year Boxing Day was on the day after Christmas, and most properly so. Why oh why ~~oh why~~

Ever since ~~Neanderthal man~~ ~~Napoleon~~ Bonaparte was never blown apart

29 Tuesday

9.00 Hospital → 291 2777

Tell Doctor: Both ends went in the night
Pilchard?

December

30 Wednesday

12.00 Pie in
12.25 Pie out

31 Thursday

New Year
Resolutions

1. Become millionaire
2. Tidy room.
3. Buy other slipper

27. Marriage

Put the slippery soap
On the slippery slope!

Set alarm for 12.00 midnight

January

1 Friday

A brand spanking New Year
Clean and shiny and
sparkling and lovely

1993
GLINT
GLEAM

DURA GLIT

SHIRLEY BASSEY
9.00 Ch4 ???

10,000 watts

2 Saturday

3 Sunday

January

4 Monday

9.40 Buy new swimming trunks.

11.00 Try Trunks (POOL)

5 Tuesday

10.00 Report Police Station (re. Trunks coming off)

Letter of Apology

TO: St. Bernadette's School for Girls.
Hampstead Road London NW1

Dear ~~Lo~~ Headmistress

Can't apologise enough for awful incident in front of your young women. ~~~~ ~~~~ My ~~bottom was clean~~

4.00 Post Box

Januar

6 Wednes

Dear Mr Bean
Rent when I get
home (Sat).
Mrs Wicket

SWINDON BY NIGHT

Mr Bean c/o Mrs Wicket
'Daffodils'
12 Arbor Rd
London
N10

1ST

7 Thursday

AAAAAAAAAAAAAAAAAAAAAAAAAAAAAAASCHHHH!!!!!

January

8 Friday

4.00 Bottom Problem

9 Saturday

7.45 Keep Fit with thin woman (ITV)

9.00 20 Press Ups
20 Sit Ups
20 Pull Ups
20 Jump Ups

10 Sunday

9.00 20 Press Ups
20 Sit Ups
20 Pull Ups
20 Jump Ups

That one with the fat girl 8.00 BBC2

January

11 Monday

9.00 ~~20~~ 10 Press Ups
~~20~~ 10 Sit Ups
~~20~~ 10 Pull Ups
~~20~~ 10 Jump Ups

10.00 Library

Try to get: "Guns Of Navarone"

"His Body Was In Bits"
by Zak Brood

Cliff

"Death Is Frequently Unexpected"
(Z. Brood)

12 Tuesday

9.00 ~~20~~ 4 Press Ups
~~20~~ 4 Sit Ups
~~20~~ 4 Pull Ups
~~20~~ 4 Jump Ups

2.30 Go back and peek at Librarian
(re. Marriage)

Wobble Dobble Fobble Bobble

January

13 Wednesday

9.00 20 Press Ups
20 Sit Ups
20 Pull Ups
20 Jump Ups

10.00 Peek at Librarian

Irma something

14 Thursday

~~9.00 20 Press Ups~~
~~20 Sit Ups~~
~~20 Pull Ups~~
~~20 Jump Ups~~

NO NO
NO NO NO
NO
NOOOOOOOO NO
NO

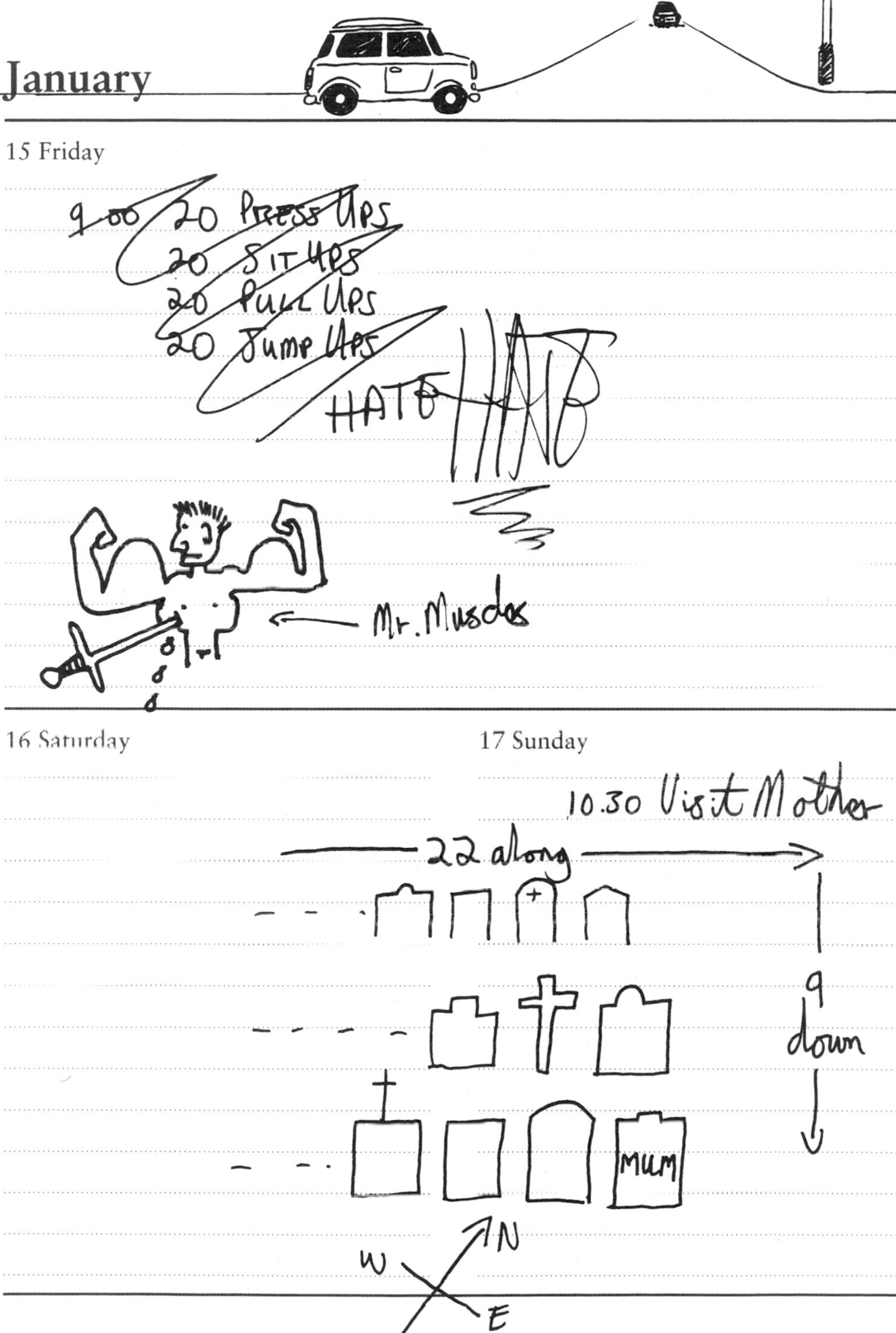

January
15 Friday
9.00 20 Press Ups
20 Sit Ups
20 Pull Ups
20 Jump Ups
HATE
HATE
Mr. Muscles
16 Saturday
17 Sunday
10.30 Visit Mother
22 along
9 down
MUM
N
W
E
S

January

18 Monday

Ring Irma Gobb
(Library 658 4890)

19 Tuesday

12.15 Lunch in PARK
12.25 Leave Park (Too much Poo)

4.00 Shops: Carpet Shampoo
Pot Pourri

January

20 Wednesday

9.15 Park

STILL ~~too~~ much Poo in Park

DOG DEVICE

CORK

© Mr. Bean

21 Thursday

Ring Inspector Morse

January

22 Friday

Dear Inspector Morse
There's so much poo in our Park you wouldn't believe it. Can you come and investigate?

I will gladly help you. I have a good ~~[illegible]~~ set of spanners

Mr. Bee Bee Bean ©

23 Saturday

That loud one with the beard 630 ITV

24 Sunday

Vicar out all day

January

25 Monday

10.00 Library

Take back: Guns of Nav.
2 x Z. Brood

Take out: "Gone with the Wind" (ROMANCE)
"Stand and Deliver"
(Autobiog. of Mollie Saxton, Midwife)
"His blood ran freely" by Zak Brood

26 Tuesday

MR. BEAN
invites you to a Party at
The Park (non-Coin-Op Toilets)

DISASTER IF WET

BRING A SANDWICH (TWO IF YOU'RE FAT)

Send to Irma

January

27 Wednesday

4.45 Ring Irma Gobb

Put Cat out ~~of its misery~~

28 Thursday

4.45 Ring Gobb

January

29 Friday

1.30 Wash Spanners

4.45 Get Gobb

30 Saturday

Irma Gobb
Has got a Job
In a busy Library
She does her Job
(Does Irma Gobb)
In a Library north of Highbury
Irma Gobby
Who's got this Job
Somewhere north of Highbury
Is the same old Irma Gobb
Whose hands are thin and Fibrey

31 Sunday

Bibbey

February

1 Mond

PLAZA CINEMA

SCREEN1

SNOW WHITE

12.00. 2.30. 4.50. 7.10. 9.30.

SCREEN3

THE WIZARD OF OZ

12.10. 2.30. 4.50. 7.10. 9.20.

SCREEN2

TARKA THE OTTER

12.30. 3.10. 5.40. 8.00. 10.20.

SCREEN4

UP NURSE, DOCTOR!

3.30. 5.50. 8.10. 10.20.

RATZY CINEMA

SCR

Romance?

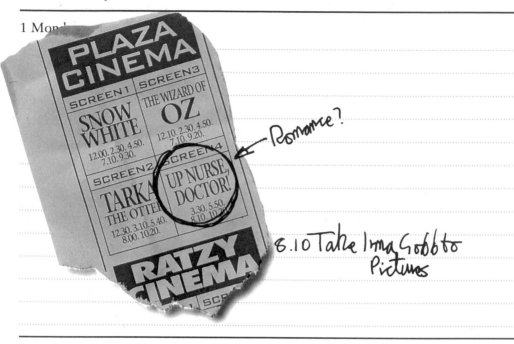

8.10 Take Irma Gobbo to Pictures

2 Tuesday

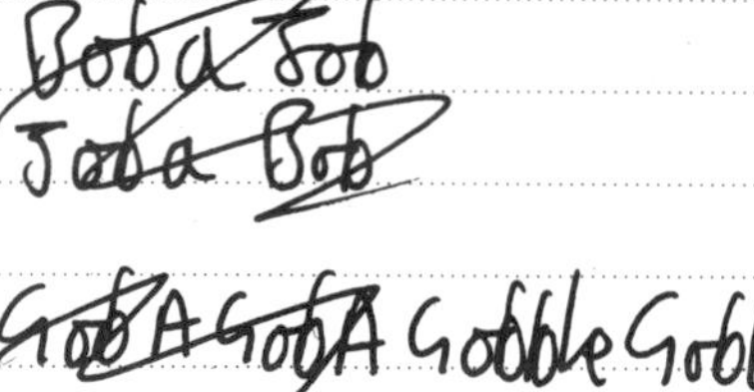

February

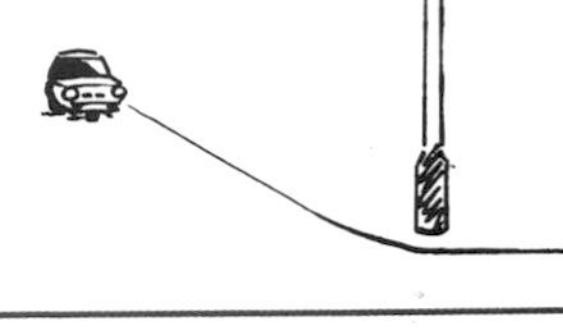

3 Wednesday

9.00 Ring Gobb

10.00 Ring Gobb

11.00 Ring Gobb

12.00 Ring Gobb

1.00 Ring Gobb

Who is Gobb?

4 Thursday

8.30 Ring Gobb
8.45 Ring Gobb
9.00 Ring Gobb
9.15 Ring Gobb
9.30 Ring Gobb
9.45 Ring Gobb
10.00 Ring Gobb
10.05 Ring Gobb
10.30 Ring Gobb
11.00 Ring Gobb
11.15 Ring Gobb
11.30 Ring Gobb

11.30 Ring Gobb
11.45 Ring Gobb
12.00 Ring Gobb
12.15 Ring Gobb
12.30 Ring Gobb
12.45 Ring Gobb
1.00 Ring Gobb
1.15 Ring Gobb
1.30 Ring Gobb
1.45 Ring Gobb
2.00 Ring Gobb
2.15 Ring Gobb

2.30 Ring Gobb
2.45 Ring Gobb
3.00 Ring Gobb
3.15 Ring Gobb
3.30 Ring Gobb
3.45 Ring Gobb
4.00 Ring Gobb
4.15 Ring Gobb
4.30 Ring Gobb
4.45 Ring Gobb
5.00 Ring Gobb
5.15 Ring Gobb
6.00 Ring Gobb
6.15 Ring Gobb
6.30 Ring Gobb

February

5 Friday

HATE HATE
HATE
HATE
HATE HATE
HATE
HATE HATE
HATE HATE
HATE
HATE

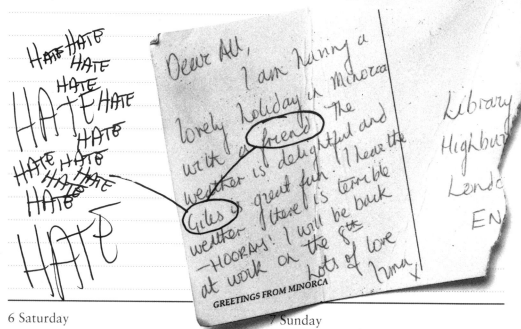

Dear All,
I am having a lovely holiday in Minorca with a friend. The weather is delightful and Giles is great fun. I hear the weather there is terrible — HOORAY! I will be back at work on the 8th
Lots of love
Irma x

Library
Highbu
Lond
EN

GREETINGS FROM MINORCA

6 Saturday

10.00 SMITHS DO-IT-ALL
EITHER SNIPER RIFLE
OR ROPE
SHEATH KNIFE
STRICHNENE
MOUSETRAP?

7 Sunday

February

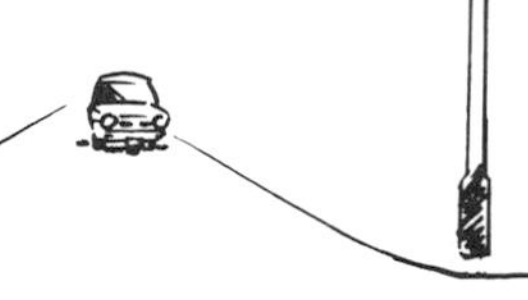

8 Monday

Hurt Flay Rip
Slash Gouge
Hit
Stab

If I put a bomb under Giles
He will go for miles and miles
And miles and miles and miles and miles
and MILES

GILES

HEAVEN ×

HELL ✓

9 Tuesday

9.30 Crimewatch UK BBC1
(Ideas)

February

10 Wednesday

2.45 Report to Police Station

METROPOLITAN POLICE your ref:
RECEIPT
our ref:

Surrendered Goods

1 BRNO .22 AIRRIFLE
1 10" KNIFE
1 SMOKE CANISTOR
3 MOUSE TRAPS
1 lt. ARALDITE
10 m. ROPE

P.C. R. Lewis

The above items have been confiscated pending a decision by local magistrates

Go to bed
zzzzzzzzzzzzzzzzzz

11 Thursday

Wake up

2.00—2.10 Sunny

I love P.C. Lewis xxx

February

12 Friday

~~Grow Beard~~ NO
Buy Fudge YES ✓✓✓ ✓✓✓ ✓✓✓

13 Saturday

Roses are red
Violets are blue
You were Miss Gobb
And I was Mr.

~~Goo~~
~~spew the Moo~~
~~Foomanchoo~~
~~Who? goo~~
True ✓✓

14 Sunday St Valentine's Day

No card

Samaritans
071 2367425

10.00 Put Out Bin

February

15 Monday

16 Tuesday

February

17 Wednesday

18 Thursday

February

19 Friday

20 Saturday

21 Sunday

February

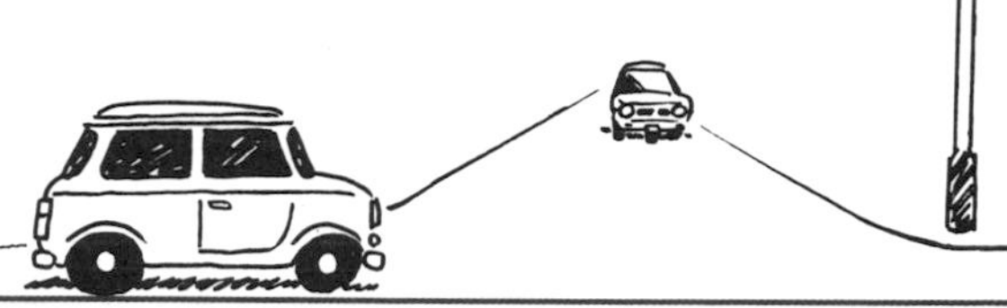

22 Monday

23 Tuesday

February

24 Wednesday

25 Thursday

FOUND DIARY!!
1.15 Soup
Hiphip hoozar
Hiphip haha
Yipee Yippee Bippee
Bippee
HAPPINESS

February

26 Fr[illegible]ay

No 3.

Dear Mr Bean,
We haven't met yet but
I have just moved into No 3
down the hall. Enclosed is
your diary which I found
today by the bins in the porch.
I would very much like to
call to make your aquaintance
and perhaps to pick up the
reward you mentioned on
the first page?

SHUT UP!

Man in No 3.

Avoid Man in No. 3

27 Satur[illegible]

N.B. Man in No. 3

N.B. Man in No. 3

March

1 Monday

Shops: Farty Cushion
False Dung
Funny hat
Celery

Those two men in that house 8.30 ITV

AVOID

IN

2 Tuesday

Coming Home?

March

3 Wednesday

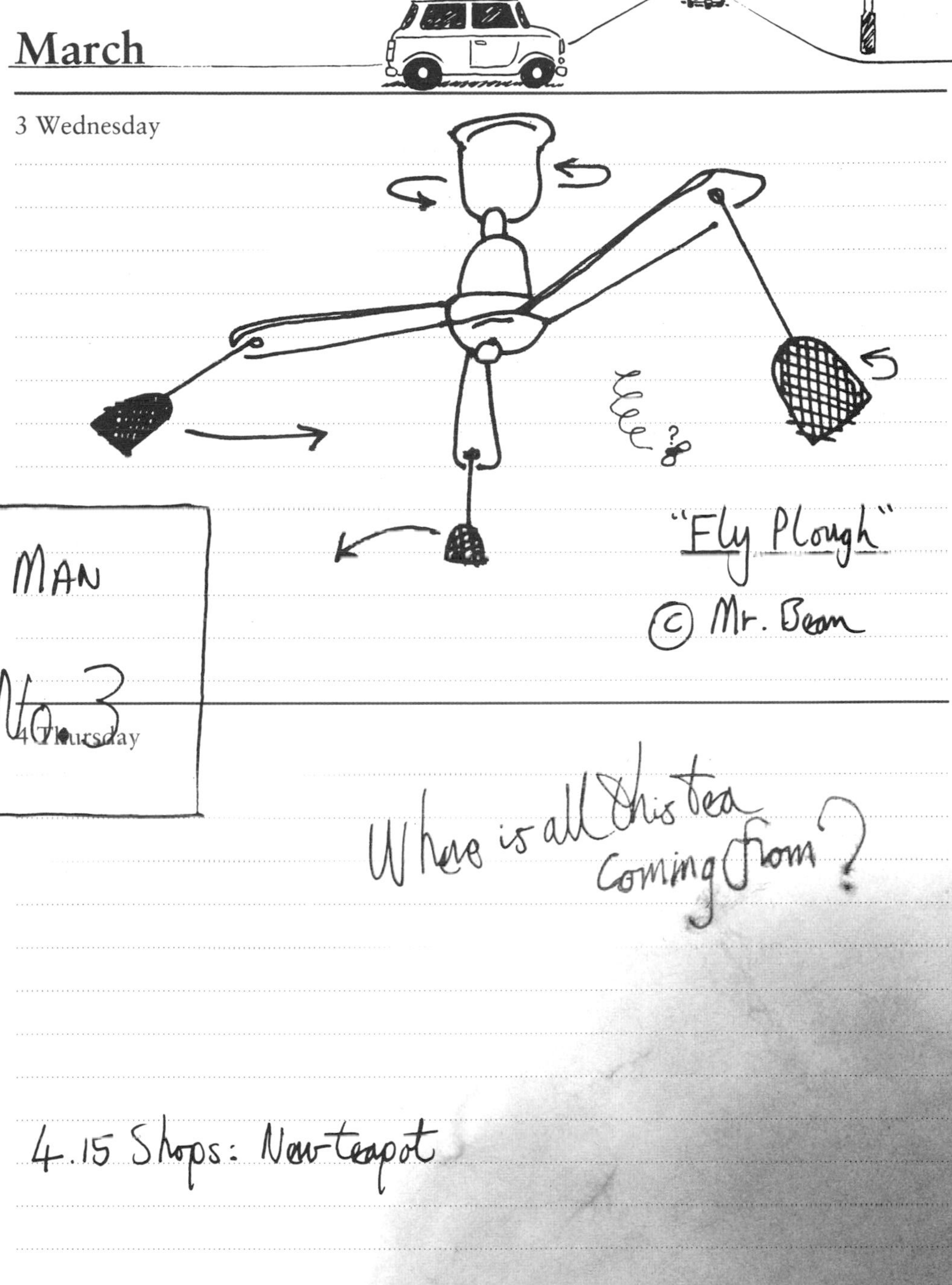

4 Thursday

Where is all this tea coming from?

4.15 Shops: New teapot

March

5 Friday

9.00 N.B. Order Flowers
for Grandad

2.00 Ring Grandma AAARGH!

RING FLORIST
RING FLORIST

Funny Man with wart 10.00 ITV

6 Saturday

9.00 RING FLORIST

7 Sunday

9.00 RING FLORIST

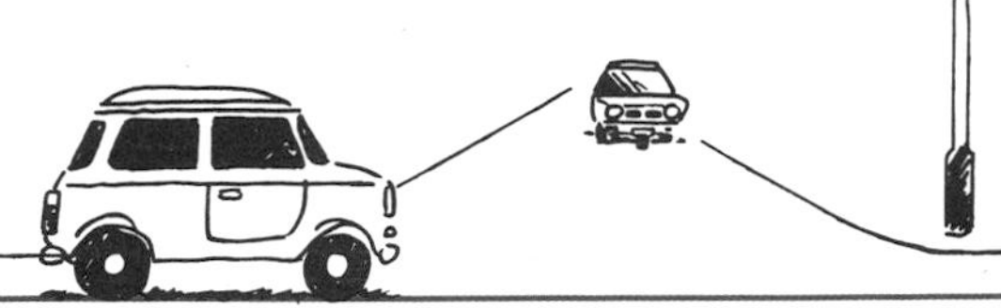

March

8 Monday

⟹ GRANDAD'S 90th BIRTHDAY (QUITE AMAZING REALLY)

RING FLORIST : CHANGE MESSAGE

3pm Grandad Funeral

9 Tuesday

Send off for Shirley Bassey Mug (Large)

to: Shirley's Mug (Large)
P.O. Box J203
Swindon
Wilts. SN43 7PZ

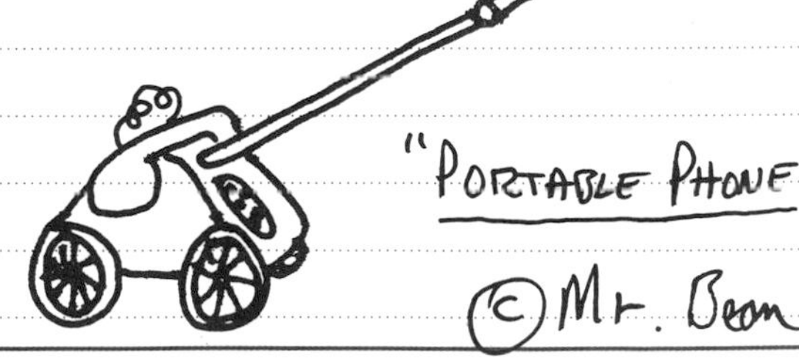

"PORTABLE PHONE"

© Mr. Bean

March

10 Wednesday

3.00pm Ring Irma Gobb – leave funny noises on Answering Machine (sobbing?)

11 Thursday

PINK TICKET NO 77

KEEP IT SAFE

Draw: 27 March

GRAND RAFFLE

In Aid of Police Benevolent Fund

1st Prize:

A Week in the Bahamas

2nd Prize:

Dinner for Two at Pizza Hut

March

12 Friday

THE FLOWER

PETAL

MIDDLE BIT

7.30 Botany Club

13 Saturday

LEAF

OTHER LEAF

GROUND

LITTLE ROOTS

ROOTS

WORM

14 Sunday

March

15 [Monday]

could end up escaping for a week somewhere.

VIRGO

(Aug 22nd - Sept 22nd)

It could be time to retile that bathroom. You will receive shattering news on 27th March, possibly regarding the number 77.

LIBRA

(Sept 22rd - Oct 23rd)

All your money worries will end soon when you get a big windfall, possibly from the pools

GOOD OMEN OR WHAT?

12 DAYS TILL RAFFLE

16 Tuesday

8.15 Rajpoot Tandoori
(Table for One)

March

17 Wednesday St Patrick's Day

Shops: Loo paper (x6)

TEN DAYS

MURPHY'S

PALE STREET

LUKE'S PASSAGE

Avoid Murphy's Bar

18 Thursday

NINE DAYS

FRAZZLE

FRAZZLE

JACKET

BAHAMAS

"RAFFLE PRIZE"

© Mr. Bean (no copycats)

March

19 Friday

EIGHT
DAYS

10.30 Building Society
Take all money out
Put no money in

Holiday shopping: Shirts
Socks
Biscuits
Vaseline

Marmalade?

20 Saturday

SEVEN
DAYS

Buy holiday
shoes

21 Sunday

SIX
DAYS

NO shops open
NO shopping
(except Vaseline)

OATH OATH
OATH!

Corydalis Lutea

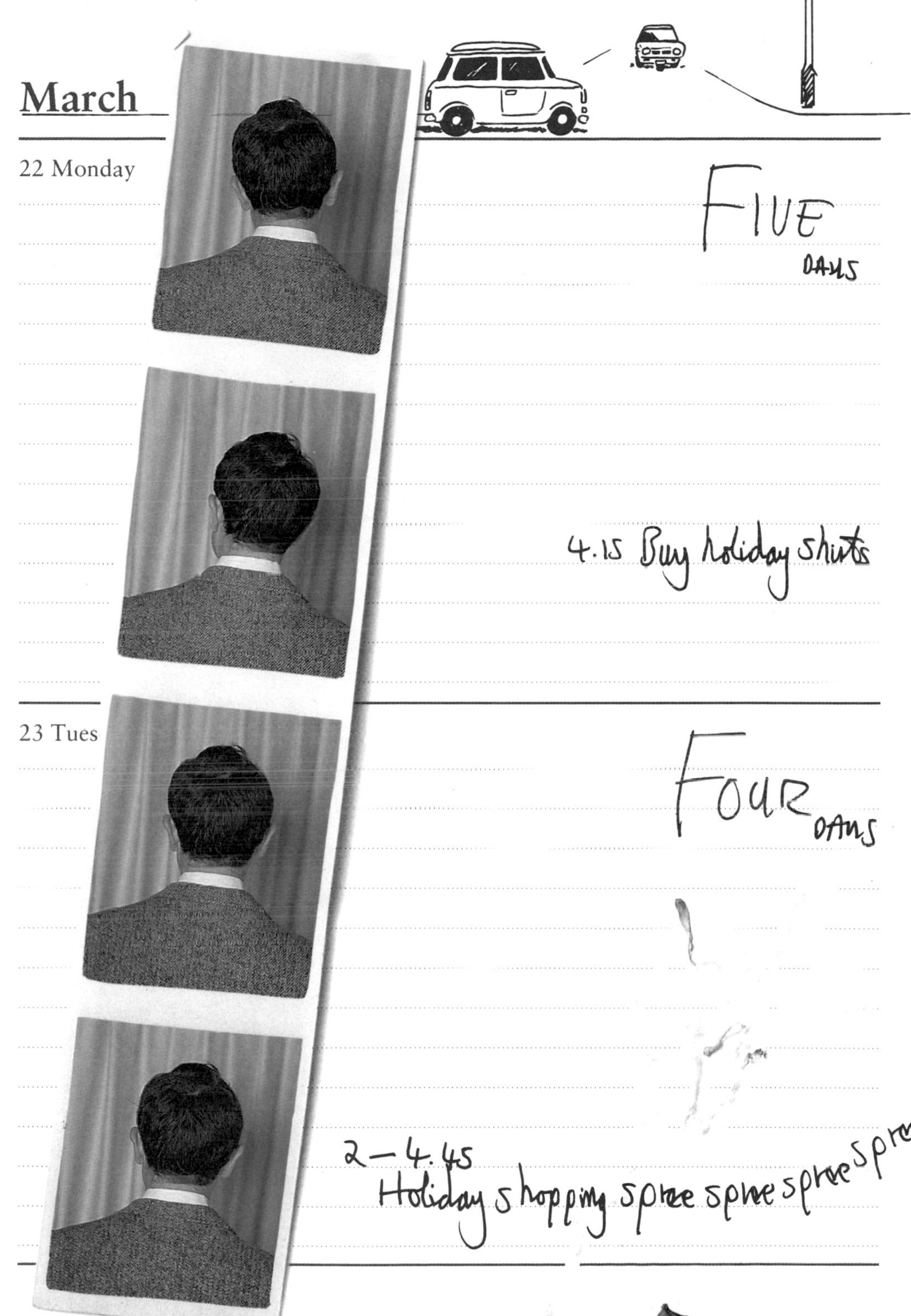

March

22 Monday

FIVE DAYS

4.15 Buy holiday shirts

23 Tues

FOUR DAYS

2–4.45
Holiday shopping spree spree spree spre

March

24 Wednesday

3

Buy holiday socks ✓

25 Thursday

2

Ring Building Soc
-No Money

Buy holiday celery ✓

If △ + ◎ + !!! + ɯ = ⊛

and Ⲡ + ✿ — ⊡ = ⩓

What is ⊡ ?

MAD MAD
MAD MAD

(4 April)

March

26 Friday

FINAL CHECKLIST: MOSQUITO STUFF
FILM
CROCODILE KNIFE
SNAKE GREASE
SPOON

~~Buy~~ Buy holiday underpants (both types)

ooh!

27 Saturday

10.55 Cross Fingers

11.00 RAFFLE DRAW
St. Andrew's Church Hall

BLAST OFF

28 Sunday

~~Travel to Barbados on plane~~

March

29 Monday

30 Tuesday

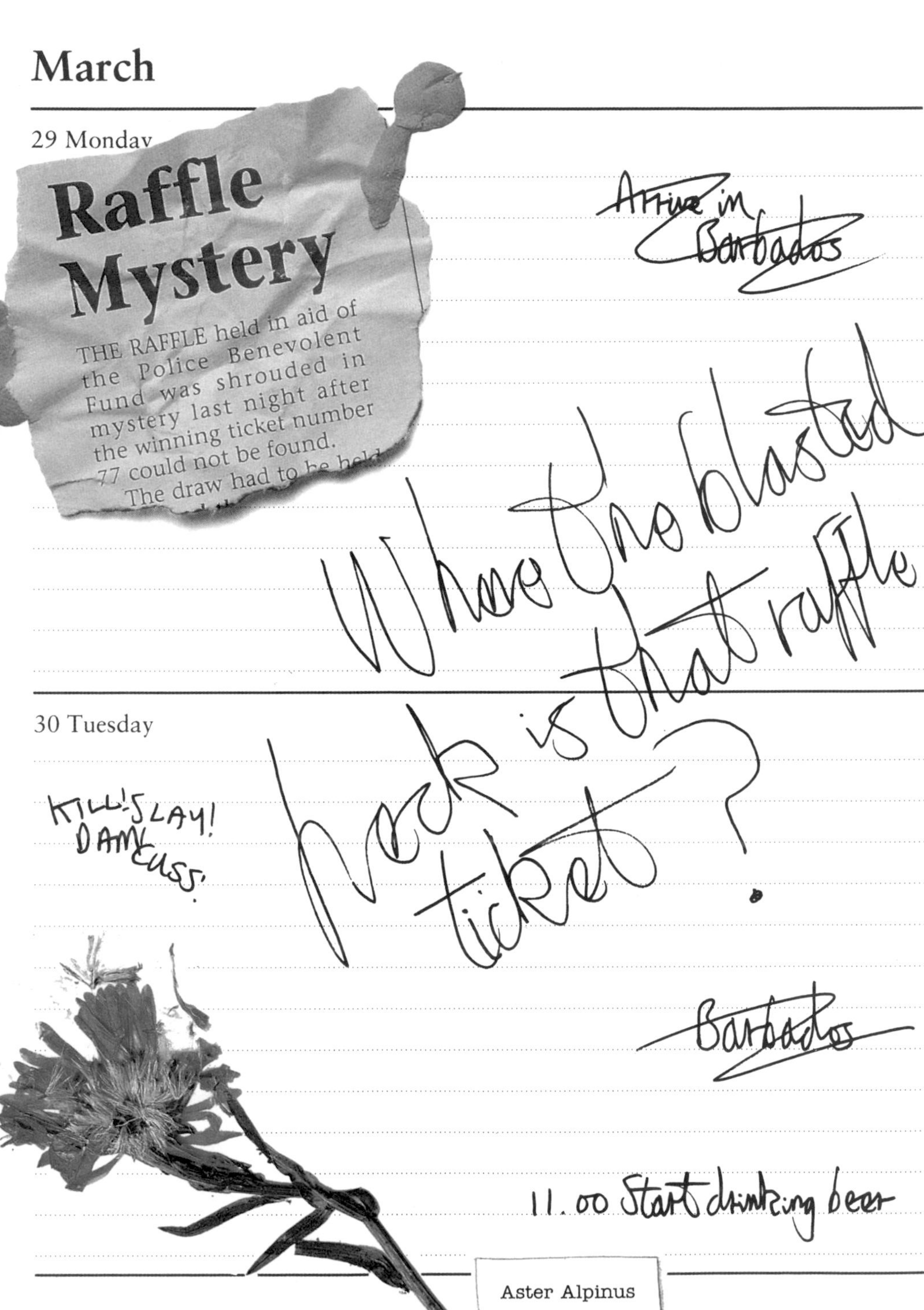

Raffle Mystery
THE RAFFLE held in aid of the Police Benevolent Fund was shrouded in mystery last night after the winning ticket number 77 could not be found. The draw had to be held
Arrive in Barbados
Where the blasted heck is that raffle ticket?
KILL! SLAY! DAMN! CUSS!
Barbados
11.00 Start drinking beer

Aster Alpinus

March/April

31 Wednesday

Drink beer all day

~~Barbados~~

~~4-8~~ POLICE Station Help

Samaritans
2367925

and all night

1 Thursday April Fool's Day

~~Barbados~~

11.45
No. 3.
Dear Mr Bean,
A parcel arrived for you while you were out. I have it with me.

Man in No. 3.
(down hall).

11.15 Man out – try later

2.10 No Man

4.42 No man

April

2 Friday

~~Barbados~~

Where oh WHERE is Shirley Bassey mug?

Ring Swindon.

D. Plumb
Private Investigator
799

Try man in No. 3

~~7.30 Botany Club~~ Too depressed

3 Saturday

~~Barbados~~

Send back Cliff Richard mug. GET OUT CLIFF COME IN Shirley WHERE ARE YOU???

4 Sunday

~~Barbados~~

O = □ + O ✓

Try man in No. 3.

April

5 Monday

~~Barbados~~

Dear Mr. Plumb

I am distraught beyond measure. I have lost a raffle ticket No. 77 and I don't know where to put myself or what to do. I have lost all sense of direction and have forgotten how to make tea, even with a tea bag which is so simple really isn't it? I last saw the ticket in my hand on March 11th. I don't know where it is. I'm sure I put it somewhere but now somebody called Caroline has gone to Barbados.

6 Tuesday

~~Barbados~~

HATE
HATE HATE HATE
HATE

CAROLINE

Snakes

SSSSS

SSSSS

NO ESCAPE

PLAN VIEW

Ring Samaritans 236 7925
re. Raffle crisis

April

7 Wednesday

~~Barbados~~

8.30 Banana

No. 3.

Dear Mr Bean,
I know you have been
knocking on my door,
but I have been ignoring
you because there is
no parcel!
APRIL FOOL!!

Man in No. 3
(down hall).

6.00 No Man

8 Thursday

~~Barbados~~ [illegible]

HELP

April

9 Friday Good Friday

6.15 Steal Milk (No.3)

~~Barbados~~

Send back Des O'Connor mug.

SEEDS: ~~Pansies~~ NO
Deadly Nightshade ✓
Widow's Misery ✓
Nasturtium ×
Love Lies Bleeding ✓

7.30 Botany Club

10 Saturday

~~Barbados~~

10.10 Goringe's (seeds)

11.00 Plant seeds

8.10 All About Terrapins
(David Atten~~burgh~~borough)
BBC2

11 Sunday Easter Day

Boiled Egg

Seeds growing

April

12 Monday   Easter Monday

Terrapin Budget:

Glass tank	£69–95	
Water	£ 0–00	
Filter	£ 15–95	
Heater	£ 25–50	
Gravel	£8–00	from shop
	£0–00	from next door's drive
Weed	£2–50	from shop
	£0–00	from next door's garden
Terrapin	£0–20p	↑ CHEAP

Seeds Growing

13 Tuesday

I love Mr. Bean

Terry the Terrapin

Seeds Growing

April

14 Wednesday

Shirley Bassey mug arrives HOORAY!

Seeds growing

11.00 Lovely hot steaming mug* of Tea mmmmmmmmmmmmmmmmmmmmmmmm!

15 Thursday

Seeds still growing

10.15 Pet Shop – buy Terrapin

3pm Christening (of Terry)

* Shirley Bassey type, large

April

16 Friday

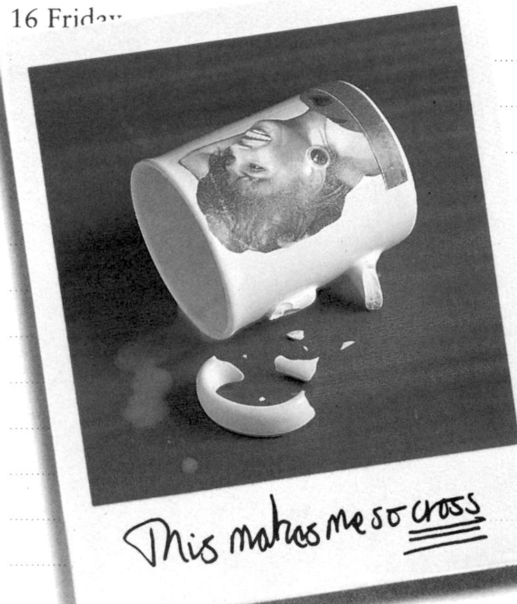

This makes me so cross

Seeds growing?

17 Saturday

10.00 Check Seeds

Oh, bosoms

18 Sunday

Seeds RUINED (DOG)

April

19 Monday

9.15 Buy seeds
9.45 Sow seeds

New seeds: Monkey Flower ✓ Red hot poker ✓✓
Baby's breath (UURGH) Stinking Helibore ✓

~~Devil in a bush~~ stupid

Plant seeds

20 Tuesday

5.45 am Creep out and steal milk

Seeds growing

Ring Samaritans
(Keep them talking)

← RUDDY MOUSE PRINTS

April

21 Wednesday Queen's Birthday Ring?

(New) Seeds should still be growing

"MOUSETRAP MK.1"

© Mr. Bean

22 Thursday 5.50am Sssssssshhhhh steal more milk

Wossit
Grossit
Twissit
Fossit

Seeds growing

That really funny one 7.00 Ch.4

April

23 Friday

10.00 Check seeds

To sum up: 1. Nothing happening
2. No little green bits
3. No flowers.
4. No nothing.
5. No good.

SNAP!

25,000,000,000,000,000,000,000,000,000,000,000,000,000,000,000, TONS

CUSS CUSS CUSS CUSS CUSS

SEED MAN

24 Saturday

No. 3.

Dear Mr Bean,
Milk bottles are frequently stolen from outside my door. Can you throw any light on the matter?
Man in No. 3 (down hall).

25 Sunday

He must be really stupid

April

26 Monday

YabadabadabadabadabadabadabadabadabadabadabadabadabadabadabadabadabadabadabadOOOO!

27 Tuesday

That wrinkly man who was in that old Police programme with Inspector Morse and ran off with the leggy dancer

8.30 BBC 1

To Mr Boon

Yours,
Shirley Bassey

April/May

30 Friday

If you make a jelly in a teapot
And try to flop it out
It takes about a fortnight
To get it out the spout

1 Saturday

Mayday mayday
All around
Ship in fog
Big hooting sound

All that noise and fuss
you make
Keep it down
For goodness sake!

2 Sunday

Write to Shirley
Bassey re. her
lovely mug

(v.v.v.v.v.v.v.v.
v.v.v. important)

May

3 Monday May Day

4 Tuesday

-2-3 Give us an S S
Give us a T T
Give us a u U
Give us a p P
Give us an i I
Give us a d D
Give us an m M
Give us an a A
Give us an n N
Give us an i I
Give us an n N
Give us an n N

Give us an o O
Give us a . .
Give us a 3 3

What is that spell?

STUPID MAN IN NO 3

Kill Kill Kill

Yes Yes Yes

May

5 Wednesday

6 Thursday

Highbury District Council
Council Offices
Highbury, London N10

Mr Bean,
c/o Mrs Wickets,
Daffodils,
Room 2, 12 Arbor Road,
London N10

15th May 1993

Dear Mr Bean

Thank you very much for your letter of the 5th May concerning, as you see it, the "outrageous" shape of your toilet.

Unfortunately, the obligations of your local council extend only as far as the provision of sewage facilities in the borough, and we cannot be held responsible for the shape of any individual apparatus. Certainly the shape of the pan you describe (your drawings are returned herewith) would appear to be traditional.

I was naturally distressed to hear of the effect that this "mad toilet" is having on your mental health. Your nightmares, accompanied, as you claim, by the "banshee howls" akin to the sound of "two enmeshed chainsaws (two-stroke)" would only become the responsibility of the local authority if complaints were received from other tenants at Daffodils. This department has no record of any such correspondence.

I therefore cannot entertain your request for a Community Charge rebate, merely on the basis of the "horrifying scenes" you describe, and the blame which you directly attribute to the curvature of your lavatory.

Yours sincerely

G.M. Nuttall

7 Friday

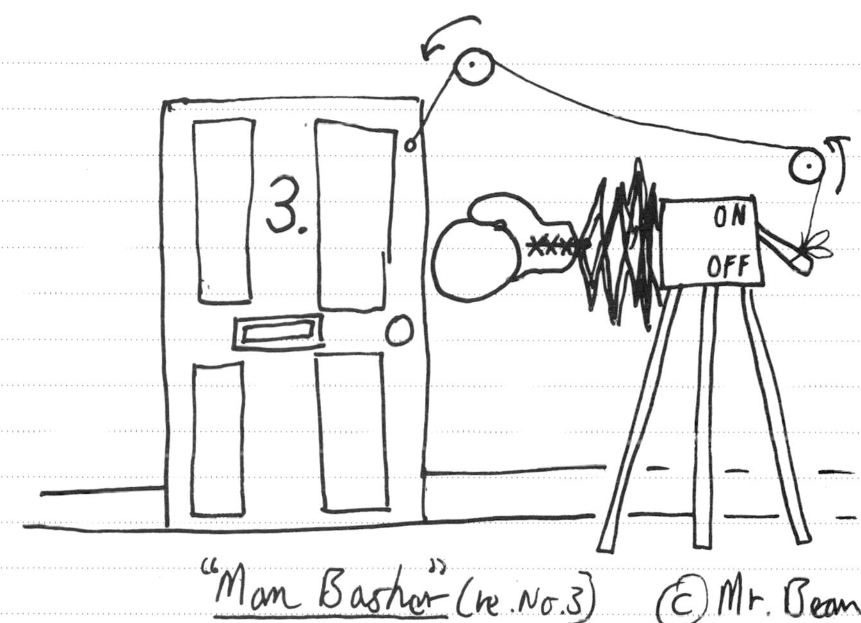

"Man Basher" (re. No. 3) © Mr. Bean

8 Saturday

TEE HEE HEE

9 Sunday

9.15 Rubbish

10.00 More Rubbish

TON

CHICKEN SOUP.

May

10 Monday

Hello Monday you look nice and fresh, but then you're always the first day aren't you?

11 Tuesday

Oh Tuesday goodness me
You've come along too, how delightful.
How do you do?

May

12 Wednesday

Ooooo! Gave me a bit of a fright there Wednesday although I should have expected you, I know, because you always bowl up on Day 3.

Sit down, do.

I've got some bitter lemon if you'd like some but nothing alcoholic I'm afraid (burp)

Oh, and Wednesday

13 Thursday

this is Thursday.

Oh, you've met, I'm sorry. You met last week?

How interesting!

Silly me.

May

14 Friday

FRIDAY where have you been?

I've been so anxious. You're always so late, you naughty boy, the week's nearly over. Honestly.

15 Saturday

Brr Brr. Brr Brr.

Ting.

Hello? Yes Mr. Beamhose. Can you not make it, Saturday? But it's the sixth day, and you're expected. Oh tish pish posh.

16 Sunday

The Lord's Day

(not my responsibility)

May

17 Monday

THE GROCER (Caught Unawares)

~~Blancmange~~
~~Stonehenge~~
Nothing rhymes with Orange
Except perhaps Lozenge

18 Tuesday

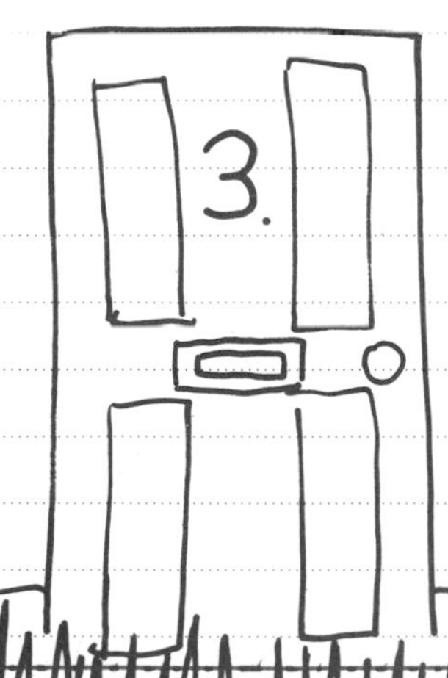

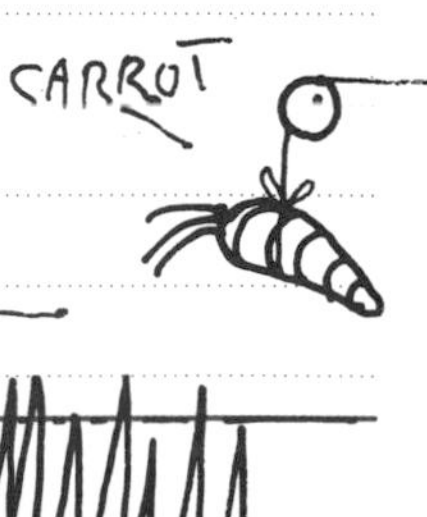

May

19 Wednesday

8.15 Get up.

Ring Irma Gobb

Join Poetry Class 7.30 (Ms. Rosemary Hosebury)

10.30 Go to bed

20 Thursday

8.15 Get up

If I had a newt
I'd have a pursuit.

Poetry research: Buy daffodils
Ring T.S. Eliot

9.30 Go to bed

May

21 Friday

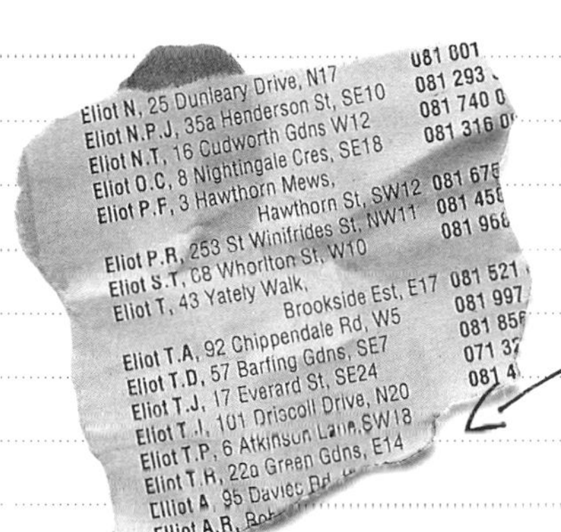

Eliot N, 25 Dunleary Drive, N17 081 001
Eliot N.P.J, 35a Henderson St, SE10 081 293
Eliot N.T, 16 Cudworth Gdns W12 081 740 0
Eliot O.C, 8 Nightingale Cres, SE18 081 316 0
Eliot P.F, 3 Hawthorn Mews, Hawthorn St, SW12 081 675
Eliot P.R, 253 St Winifrides St, NW11 081 458
Eliot S.T, 68 Whorlton St, W10 081 968
Eliot T, 43 Yately Walk, Brookside Est, E17 081 521
Eliot T.A, 92 Chippendale Rd, W5 081 997
Eliot T.D, 57 Barfing Gdns, SE7 081 856
Eliot T.J, 17 Everard St, SE24 071 37
Eliot T.J, 101 Driscoll Drive, N20 081 4
Eliot T.P, 6 Atkinson Lane, SW18
Eliot T.R, 22a Green Gdns, E14
Elliot A, 95 Davies Rd
Elliot A.R, Bo
Elliot

T.S. Eliot ex-directory?..

10.30 Go to bed (Boring)

22 Saturday

9.30 Get up (Yippee!)

10.30 Go to bed.

23 Sunday

Don't get up

If I haven't got up, then I won't have to ~~go to~~ bed

HOORAY!!

May

24 Monday

Ring Irma Gobb
And keep it clean
If you get
Answer machine

Shirley Bassey in Pro-Am Golf 8.00 BBC2

25 Tuesday

DAM DAM DAM DAM DAM DAM DAM DAM DAM DAM DAM DAM DAM DAM DAM DAM

May

26 Wednesday

Poem: Attention Mice

You'd better watch out
Cos if I see you about
You're going to end up in my mincer
Then, no mucking about
I'll scrape you all out
And do the same thing to your sister

7.30 Poetry Class

27 Thursday

"Mousetrap Mk. 2"

© Mr. Bean

May

28 Friday

9.00 Buy Fish

Leave out all day

29 Saturday

Leave out all day

30 Sunday

Really smelly now

3.

Tee hee

May/June

31 Monday

Up at nine
Out by ten
Drive to town
Drive home again

Those two men in that house 8.00 ITV

1 Tuesday

June

2 Wednesday

Picnic shopping : Tea Bag
Lettuce
Sticklebacks in Brine

1.00 Picnic in Park.

Cilla Black
Has a lack
(Out) Shirley Wirley
(Bassey)
Is a cuddly girley

7.30 Poetry Class

3 Thursday

Don't do ANYTHING today AT ALL

except go to the toilet

June

4 Friday

Terry (the Terrapin) R.I.P.

Oh Lord who giveth and taketh away, taketh away Terry and put him in a nice big tank in heaven and remember to feed him because I forgot

Amen.

5 Saturday

Give Terry's tank, water, weeds, and gravel away to somebody — Oxfam?

HELP FEED STARVING TERRAPINS ALL OVER THE WORLD

6 Sunday

Help on it's way

WHOOSH HELP

OFF

June

7 Monday

There's a poetry test
I'm sure to pass
In Ms Rosemary Hosebury's
Poetry Class
She's given us the title
"A Goddess Sublime"
Which will take no time
For the Prince of Rhyme (to do)

8 Tuesday

POETIC LICENCE
ALL
CATEGORIES
EXPIRES: 7 JUNE 1994
Mr BEAN
MALE

9.45 Turn in

June

9 Wednesday

A GODDESS SUBLIME by Mr. Bean

If there's anything in the world
That I would like to be
It's Shirley Bassey's microphone
So she could sing to me

I know she sings to everyone
When they come to hear her
But front row seats cost fifteen quid
And I would be much nearer.

Another thing that strikes me

7.30 Poetry Class

10 Thursday

About being up that close
Is that I could smell her perfume
And see right up her nose*

I know microphones get dribbled on
But so what, what the hell?
It's a perk of the job when it's Shirley's gob
And I'd get in free as well!

*N.B. Check with Ms. Hosebury – close & nose rhyme

June

1[illegible]ay

Ring Samaritans
re. drains

12 Saturday

Get up early tomorrow

13 Sunday

11.15 Forget it

June

14 Monday

11.10 Give blood

15 Tuesday

~~Dear Council~~
~~Nurse Gibby~~,

Wash out
Jam Jar

Dear Blood Man/Woman

I would like to become a blood donor and enclose, for your perusal,

June

16 Wednesday

17 Thursday

Highbury Royal Infirmary
Highbury, London N10

re: 16 June
from: Highbury Royal Infirmary

Dear Mr Bean

Although we are pleased that you have decided to become a blood donor, I'm afraid that we cannot accept donations by post. We have disposed of your blood in accordance with the conditions of the Medicines Act 1709, and your jam jar is returned herewith.

Perhaps you would like to give blood when a mobile unit visits your area? If you would like further information, please see your doctor.

Perhaps you will be seeing your doctor anyway?

Yours sincerely

Jose Manteras

Jose Manteras
Doctor

June

CRASH!

18 Friday

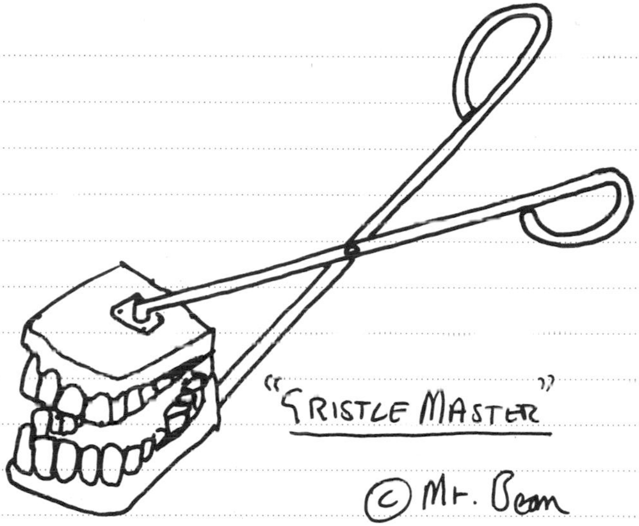

"GRISTLE MASTER"

© Mr. Bean

19 Saturday

Shops: Loaf
Butter
Egg (x2)
Spindle
Grommet

20 Sunday

Church?

June

21 Monday

Tipula Maxima

6.00 Lance Boil

22 Tuesday

9.15 Lance Boil

6.15 Ring Lance Boil

7.45 Entymology Club
↳ What is Entymology?

June

23 Wednesday

Morning: Go to Library

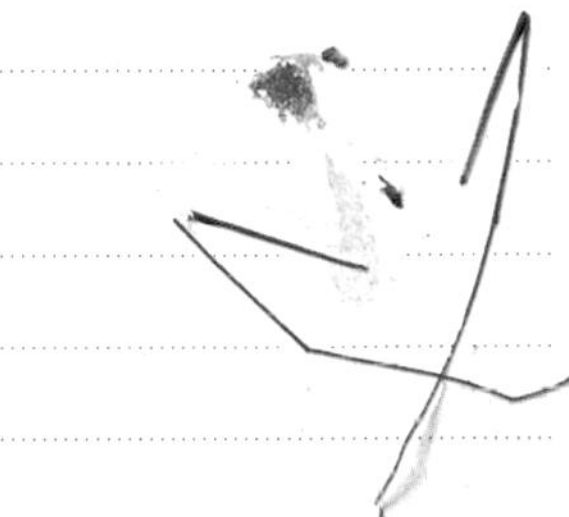

...tas -tatis f. *integer*: see ENTIRE]
...le /ɪn'taɪt(ə)l/ *v.tr.* **1 a** (usu. foll. by *to*) give (a person etc.) a just claim. **b** (foll. by *to* + infin.) give (a person etc.) a right. **2 a** give (a book etc.) the title of. **b** *archaic* give (a person) the title of (*entitled him sultan*). ▫▫ **entitlement** *n.* [ME f. AF *entitler*, OF *entiteler* f. LL *intitulare* (as IN-², TITLE)]
entity /'entɪtɪ/ *n.* (*pl.* -ies) **1** a thing with distinct existence, as opposed to a quality or relation. **2** a thing's existence regarded distinctly. ▫▫ **entitative** /-tətɪv/ *adj.* [F *entité* or med.L *entitas* f. LL *ens* being]
ento- /'entəʊ/ *comb. form* within. [Gk *entos* within]
entomb /ɪn'tu:m/ *v.tr.* **1** place in or as in a tomb. **2** serve as a tomb for. ▫▫ **entombment** *n.* [OF *entomber* (as EN-¹, TOMB)]
entomo- /'entəməʊ/ *comb. form* insect. [Gk *entomos* cut up (in neut. = INSECT) f. EN-² + *temnō* cut]
entomology /,entə'mɒlədʒɪ/ *n.* the study of the forms and behaviour of insects. ▫▫ **entomological** /-mə'lɒdʒɪk(ə)l/ *adj.* **entomologist** *n.* [F *entomologie* or mod.L *entomologia* (as ENTOMO-, -LOGY)]

← BINGO!

24 Thurs

ANGRY IRMA

TEE ~~HEE~~ HEE ~~HEE~~ HEE

June

25 Friday

11.00 MFI (Cupboard – self assembly)

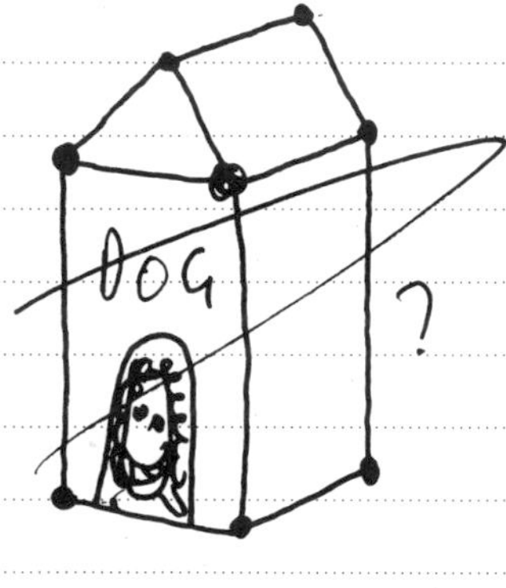

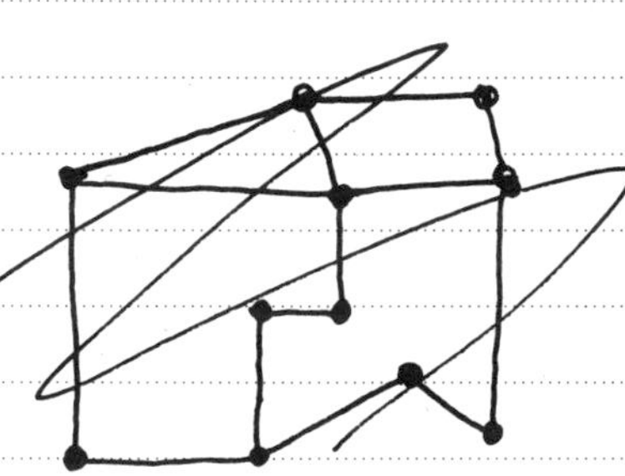

26 Saturday

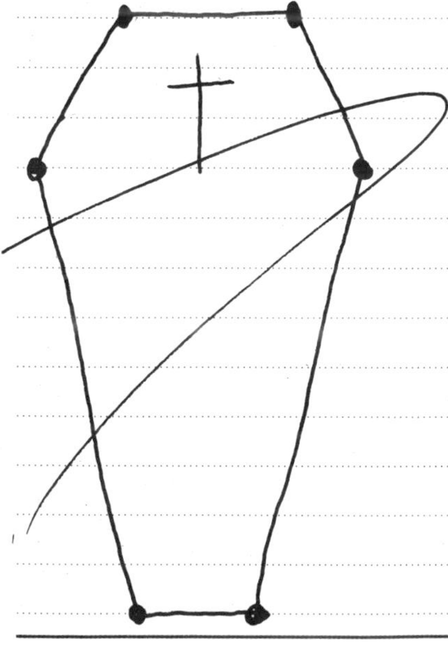

27 Sunday

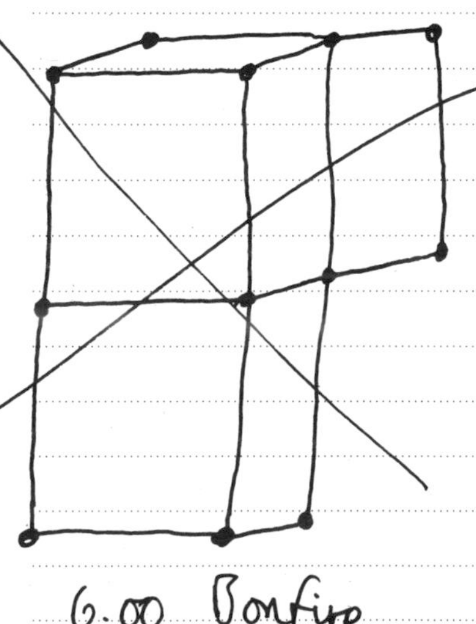

6.00 Bonfire

June

CRASH!

28 Monday

Oh what a horrible morning oh what a horrible day
I've got a horrible feeling that people just get in my way

but only ONCE

and then it's CURTAINS

for them

Heh heh heh heh heh heh heh

29 Tuesday

Yesterday up on the stairs
I caught a man unawares

I gave him a fright again today
By taking both his ears away

(You should have seen him)

7.45 Entymology Club
(Spelling 10/10)

June/July

30 Wednesday

6.00 News (BBC1) De de dom de de dommm de de dun dum dum dum do do do dum dum do do dum downnnnnn..
... This is the Six O'clock News from the BBC with thingummy Jig and what's her face...... de de dom de de dunn.

1 Thursday

Tenebrio Molitor

10.00 News at Ten (ITV)
(Pay attention)

CRASH!

July

2 Friday

Shops: Shake in Vac

12.00 Clean Jacket (Tweed)

3 Saturday

9.20 Go out
10.04 Come in
10.24 Go out again
12.10 Come in again
1.45 Go out again
2.05 Come in again
TR EYS [2.55 Go out again.
2.56 Come in again
2.57 Go out again]
4.50 Come in again
6.03 Go out again
6.43 Forget to come in again
7.00 Miss Programme
7.28 Eventually come in again

4 Sunday

CANCELLED

July

5 Monday

Ring Irma Gobb?

No, can't be bothered.

I would very much like to go to the moon, even though I don't like travel, as a rule. No language problems, and no crowding.

6 Tuesday

Also, no air.

GASP GASP GASP

9.10 Over the moon about something

7.45 Entymology Club

lots of creepy crawlies

July

7 Wednesday

Young people with ~~funny~~ horrible accents 5.40 BBC1

8 Thursday

Shopping (to service car): GREASE
OIL
EGG WHISK
~~A~~ Filter
Coffee
Gherkins
Spotting spigot

Fairy liquid
Alarm clock?
Bottle (dont lose it)

July CAR SERVICING

9 Friday

(PHOTO GUIDE)

STUFF REQUIRED

ENGINE
(LOCATION OF)

10 Saturday

CHANGE FILTER

TOP UP RADIATOR

CHANGING THE OIL

TOUCH-UP PAINTWORK

BEFORE

AFTER

CHANGE BULB IN BOOT

ALL DONE!

Entymology Club 7.45

July

14 Wednesday

OLD Getting dressed procedure: First Shirt
then Socks
then Underpants
then Trousers
then Shoes
then Tie
then Belt
BORING then Jacket

15 Thursday

NEW Getting dressed procedure:

First Shirt
then Jacket
then Tie

First Shoes
then Socks

First Trousers
then Undies
then
Stupid
Impossible
stupid
boring

First
then
then
Undies
Jacket
Tie
Mad mad
mad

First Belt
then Tie
then Shoes
then Leave House
Too rude
then Jail

July

CRASH!

16 Friday

10.45 Library Return "Gone with the Wind"
"Stand and Deliver"

Get out "Insects of Yesteryear" by E. Dalton

"The Land of Gore" by Zak Brood
"Limb from Limb" by Zak Brood
(Parts 1 & 2)

"Are you bleeding comfortably?"
(Z. Brood)

also Ask Gobb to Pictures

17 Saturday

8.10 HORROR FILM

Yes Yes
Yes

18 Sunday

10.15 Vicar (Exorcism)

Sleep with light on

July

19 Monday

Seek Professional Help.

20 Tuesday

North London
Technical College
Highbury, London N10

Mr Bean,
c/o Mrs Wickets,
Daffodils,
Room 2, 12 Arbor Road,
London N10

16th July 1993

Dear Mr Bean

I'm sure that I need not reiterate the horror and revulsion felt by all of us when you revealed your pressed insect collection. It is inhuman to murder God's creatures in this way, merely to form a macabre collection in the pages of your diary.

There has been a unanimous decision taken by our sub-committee to report your behaviour to the RSPCA, from whom I hope you will be hearing soon.

You really are a quite revolting man.

Dr Legge

Dr. Legge
Sec., Entomology Club

July

21 Wednesday

Seek Professional Help re. Nightmares

Can't sleep

22 Thursday

Can't sleep

Clossiana Euphrosyne

July

23 Friday

Smiths Do-It-All : 1 Mirror
: 1 Wodon stake

Sainsburys : 10 lbs Garlic

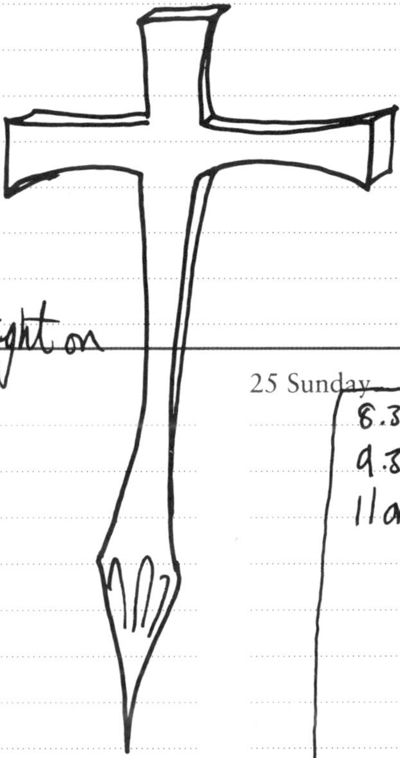

Sleep with light on

24 Saturday

Lock door
Sleep with light on

25 Sunday

8.30 Holy Communion
9.30 Family Service
11am Mattins

6.30 Evensong
(Attend religiously)

July

CRASH

26 Monday

Stay in all day

Breathe quietly

Video: The Exorcist

SSSSSSSSSssshhhhhhhhhh...

27 Tuesday

SCREAM

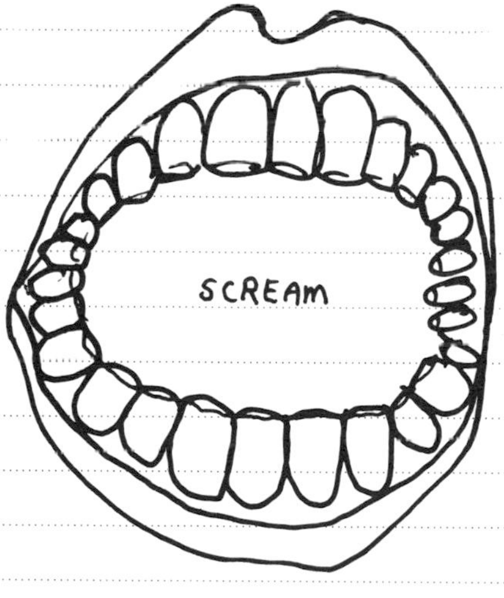

Pull myself together.

July

28 Wednesday

Close my eyes
Up tight and sing
Go away
You big bad thing!
Open them again
And shout GO AWAY

29 Thursday

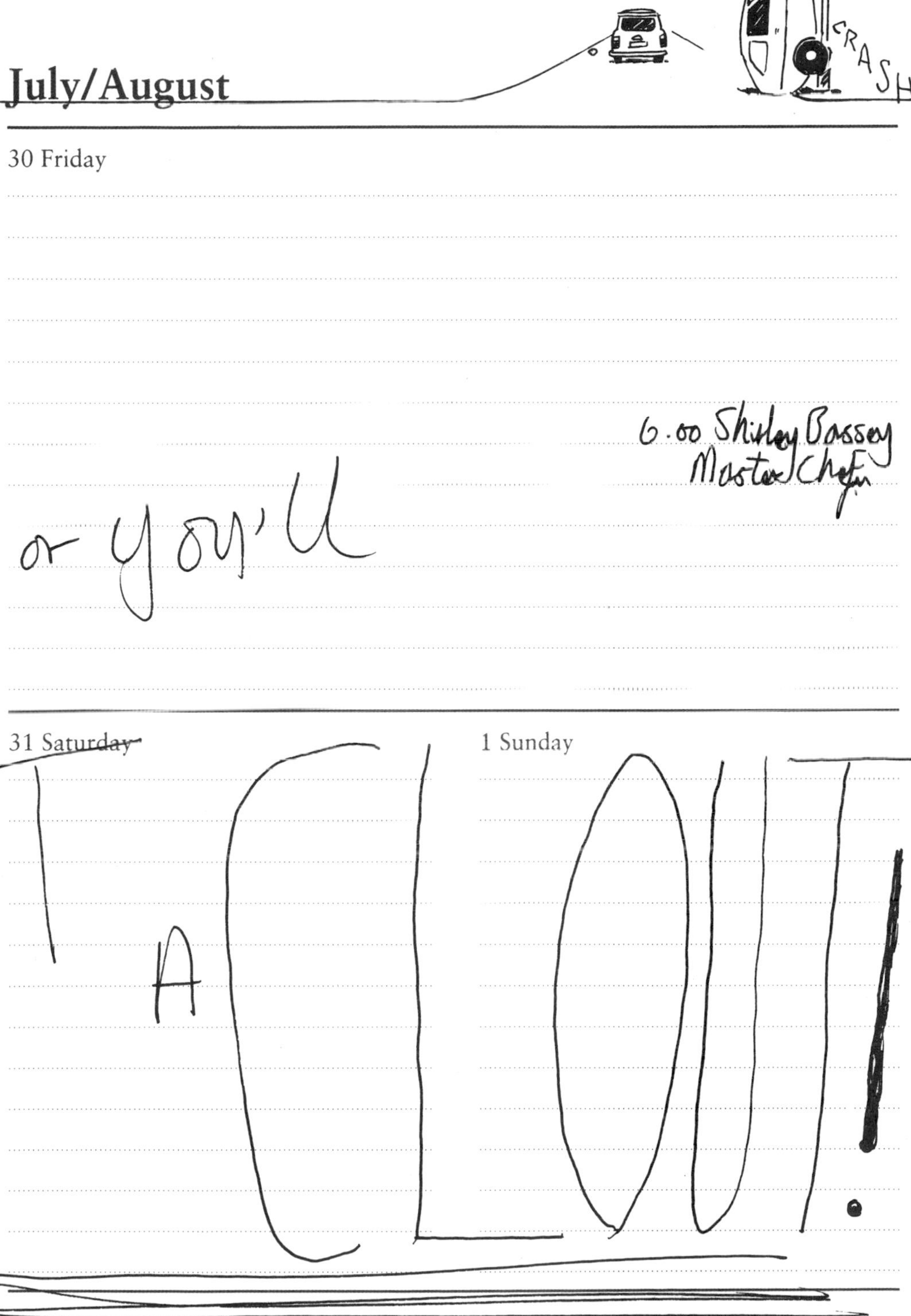
CRASH
July/August
30 Friday
6.00 Shirley Bassey
Master Chef
or you'll
31 Saturday
1 Sunday
GET A CLOUT!

August

2 Monday

Feeling much better today, thank you.

Shops: Beans
Bread

Long Johns

3 Tuesday

9.45 Mrs. Wicket (Root)

7.15 Bum something
(Mrs. Wicket?)

August

4 Wednesday

Significant disturbances.

Beans for dinner
Beans for tea
Oh windy Bean
Oh windy me

5 Thursday

Further disturbances (Bottom Dept.)

© Mr. Bean

August

6 Friday 8.30 Take Mini to Man

7 Satur

A. & G. MOTORS
10 Ugly Street, Twickenham
081 851 1590

Dear Mr Bean

thought you should know, that your mini is a Dog. we looked at it this morning. and it is completely clapped. You need a new sub frame mate and big ends and mounts and exhaust etc to name but a few. Tires are as bald as that swimmer bloke. Were talking a lot of cash. like two or three hundred also the brown stuffs everywhere (you been driving fast again!!!!!!!) No I mean the rust its terrible the car is really shot. My feet went through the floor at Sainsburys roundabout, Fred Flintstone Eat your heart out!!! Come to the garage and you better say what you want cos we're going to Rimini Tuesday

Graham

P.S. My mate thinks you're weird

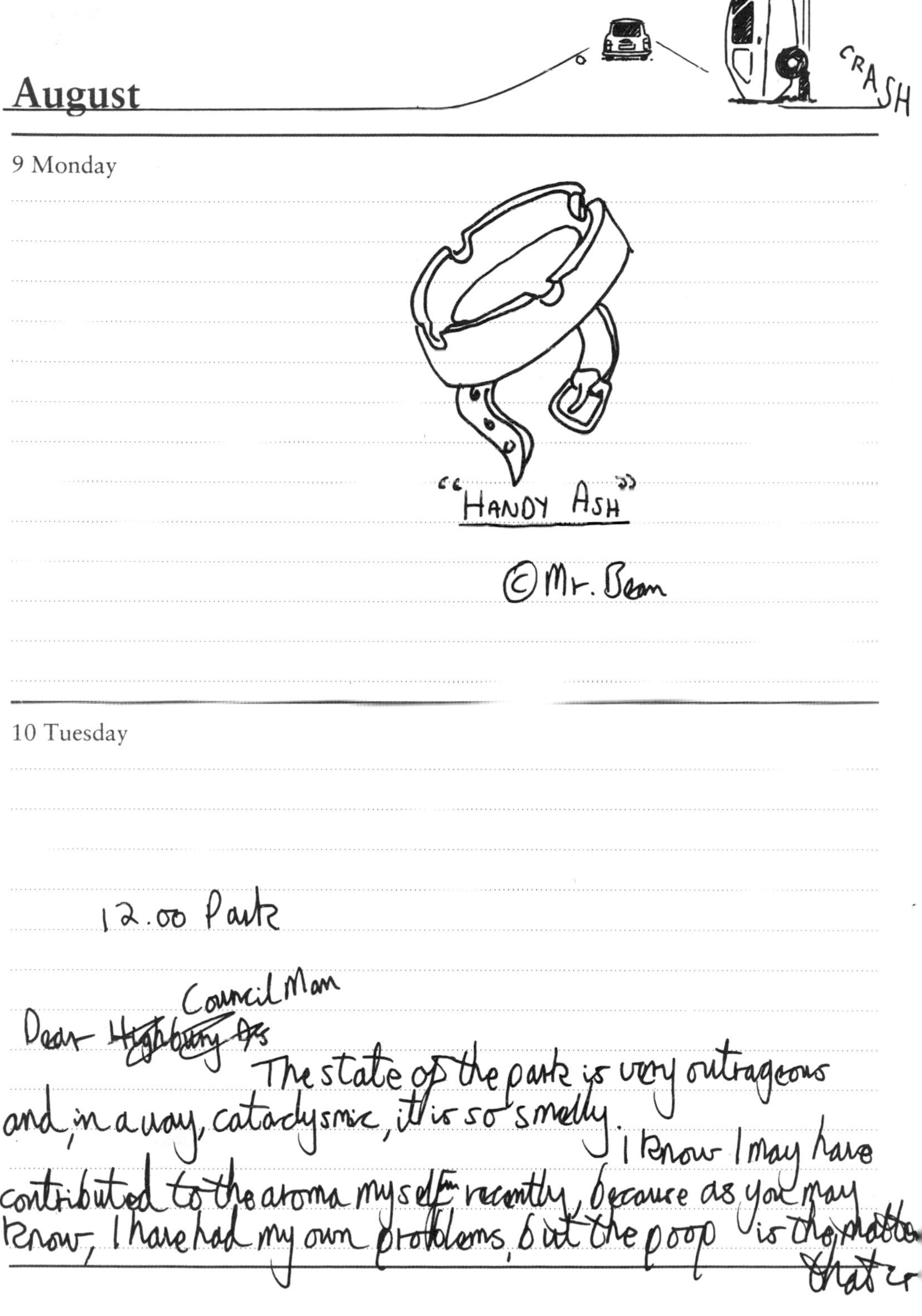

August

9 Monday

10 Tuesday

12.00 Park

Dear ~~Highbury~~ ~~Os~~ Council Man

The state of the park is very outrageous and, in a way, catadysmic, it is so smelly.

I know I may have contributed to the aroma myself recently, because as you may know, I have had my own problems, but the poop is the ~~matte~~ that is

August

11 Wednesday

12 Thursday

"Daffodils"
12 Arbor Rd.
LONDON N10

BEAN ANTI-POOP ASSOCIATION (BAPA)

Dear Resident

I hope you are well. I am fine. I am writing to ask if, like me, you are sick and tired of too much 'poop'

Dogs treat this road, and the park, like a huge toilet, which it isn't. Join BAPA and help me stamp out poop. Any dog owner caught ~~fouling our paths~~ allowing a dog to foul our paths will get a right dressing down, and further abuse.

Those responsible for more than one poop will get a punch up the bracket. (We could take it in turns)

If you are interested, please fill in this form, and send it back.

- - - - - - - - - - ✂ - - - - - - - - - -

NAME . . . .
ADDRESS . . . .
. . . .
. . . .

I think your idea is great. Signed
. . . .

August

CRASH

13 Friday

9.45 Library (Photocopier). ref. Too much poop (BAPA)

Ring Samaritans re. poop.

14 Saturday

15 Sunday

Do I like Golf?

IN →

August

16 Monday

BY APPOINTMENT TO
HER MAJESTY THE QUEEN
POOP PREVENTATIVE AND DIRT DISPOSAL
MERCHANTS BEAN ANTI-POOP ASSOCIATION

17 Tuesday

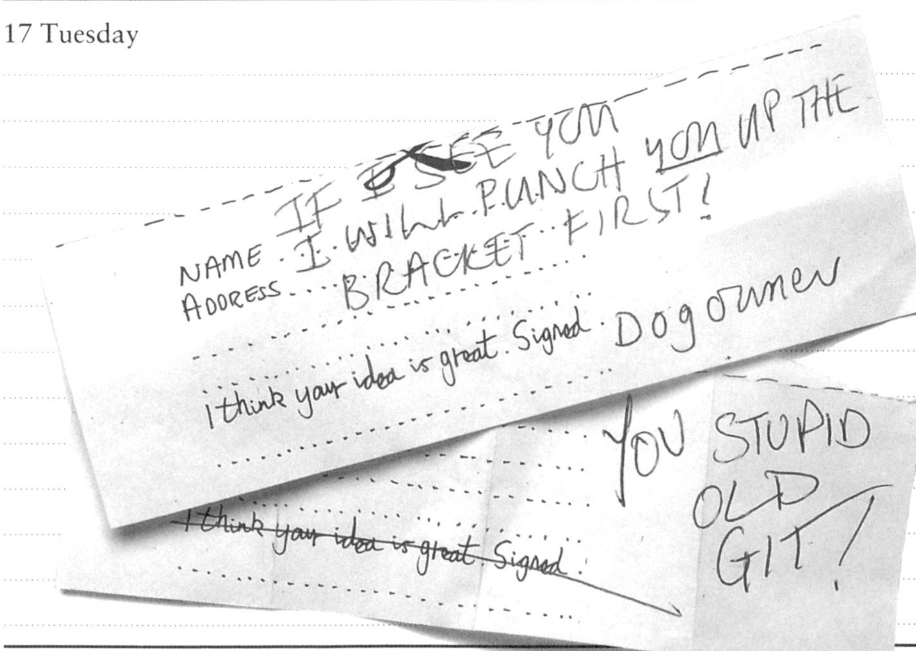

August

18 Wedne

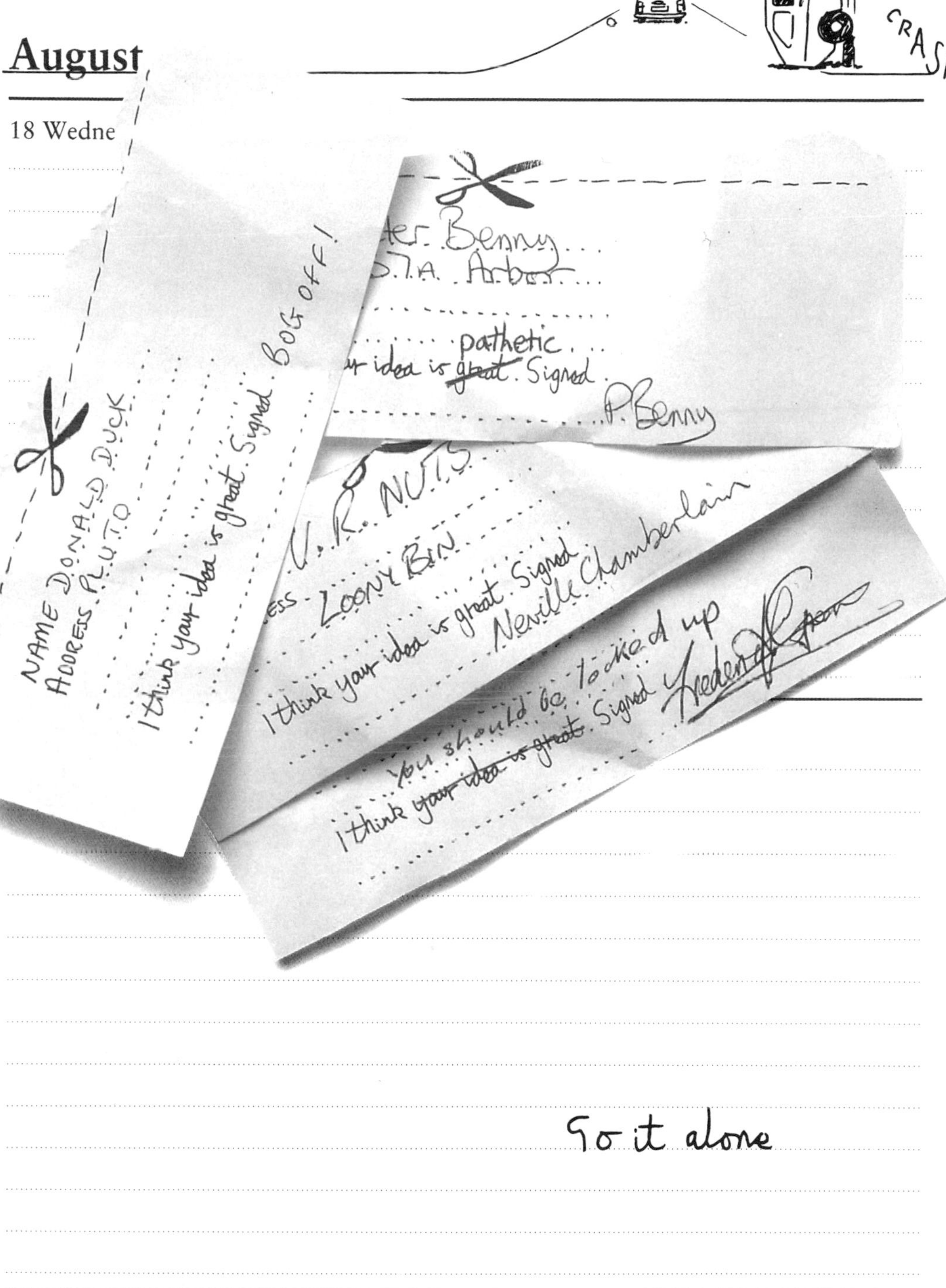

CRASH
NAME DONALD DUCK
ADDRESS PLUTO
I think your idea is great Signed BOG OFF!
ter Benny
S.T.A. Arbor
ur idea is ~~great~~ pathetic Signed
P. Benny
U. R. NUTS
ess LOONY BIN
I think your idea is great Signed
Neville Chamberlain
I think ~~your idea is great~~ you should be locked up Signed
Go it alone

August

20 Friday

21 Saturday

METROPOLITAN POLICE
4, Guildford Street
Highbury
London N10

Dear Mr. Bean

It has been drawn to our attention that you have been circulating letters to the residents in your area of the borough, complaining about the problem of dogs fouling the pavement. This is not a criminal offence in itself, but the blatant incitements to violence which are also contained therein most certainly are.

We received a complaint from a dog owner yesterday, claiming that he was recently attacked by a man answering to your description. After the complainant's pet had made an accidental deposit in the park, the attacker attempted to force the owner's nose into the excreta. This is not the kind of behaviour that upstanding citizens should have to suffer. The hooligan was also carrying a quantity of corks, with one of which he attempted to violate the dog.

If this attacker was yourself, you must appreciate that the Constabulary takes a very dim view of this kind of behaviour: if we hear of any similar incidents, or af any further letters, criminal proceedings will be brought against you.

Yours sincerely

Sgt. Ricke

Sgt. P.R.D. Rickers

August

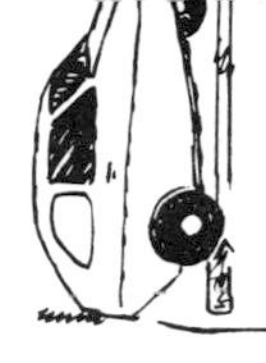

CRA

23 Monday

9.00am <u>Commence BAPA Stealth Deterrent Mk. 1</u>

Glue
Soap
Timber 24' x 1½" x 1½"
Duvet Cover
Broom handle
Bread knife

Tow bar
Pillow case
Electric Fan
Bed sheet
Screws
Nails
Horse Poop (½ Ton)

24 Tuesday

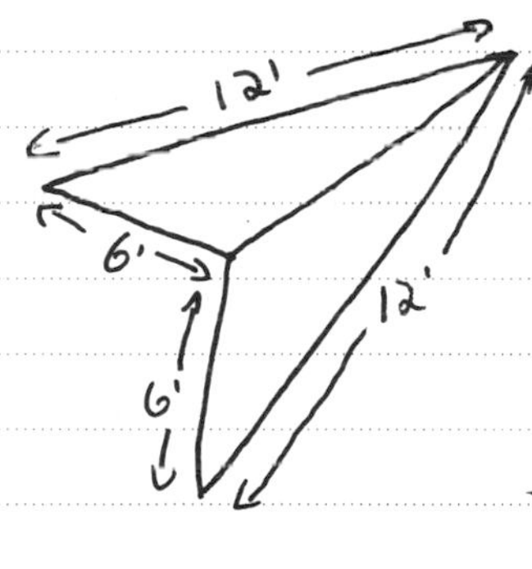

Fig.1

The fat man with the long hands 6.30 BBC1

August

25 Wednesday

Sore throat

I've got to be firmer
With Irma
If she's going to be
A long termer

Nose getting blogged

26 Thursday

Nose completely stuffed
full of snot

Chemist: Paraffin
Pipe cleaners?

4.00 Unfortunate snot accident (Mrs. Wicket)

August

27 Friday

Letter of Apology (Mrs. Wicket)

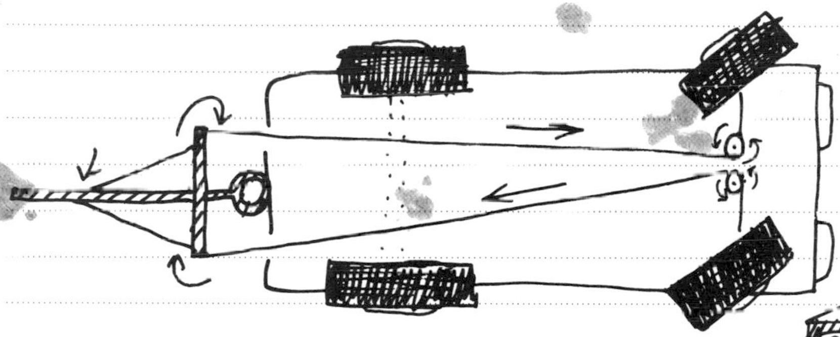

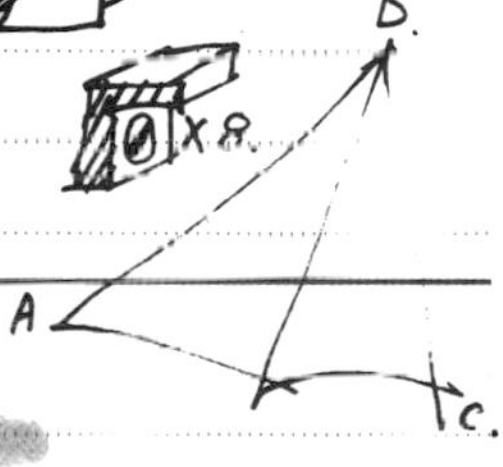

BAPA Deterrent: Fig. 2

28 Saturday

Construction to continue apace

9.00 Bonk bonk bonk

2.30 Tap tap tap tap

8.15 Kersplak Kersplak

29 Sunday

7.00 Bang bang bang bang bang bang bink OWW! Bang bang bang

August

30 Monday

31 Tuesday

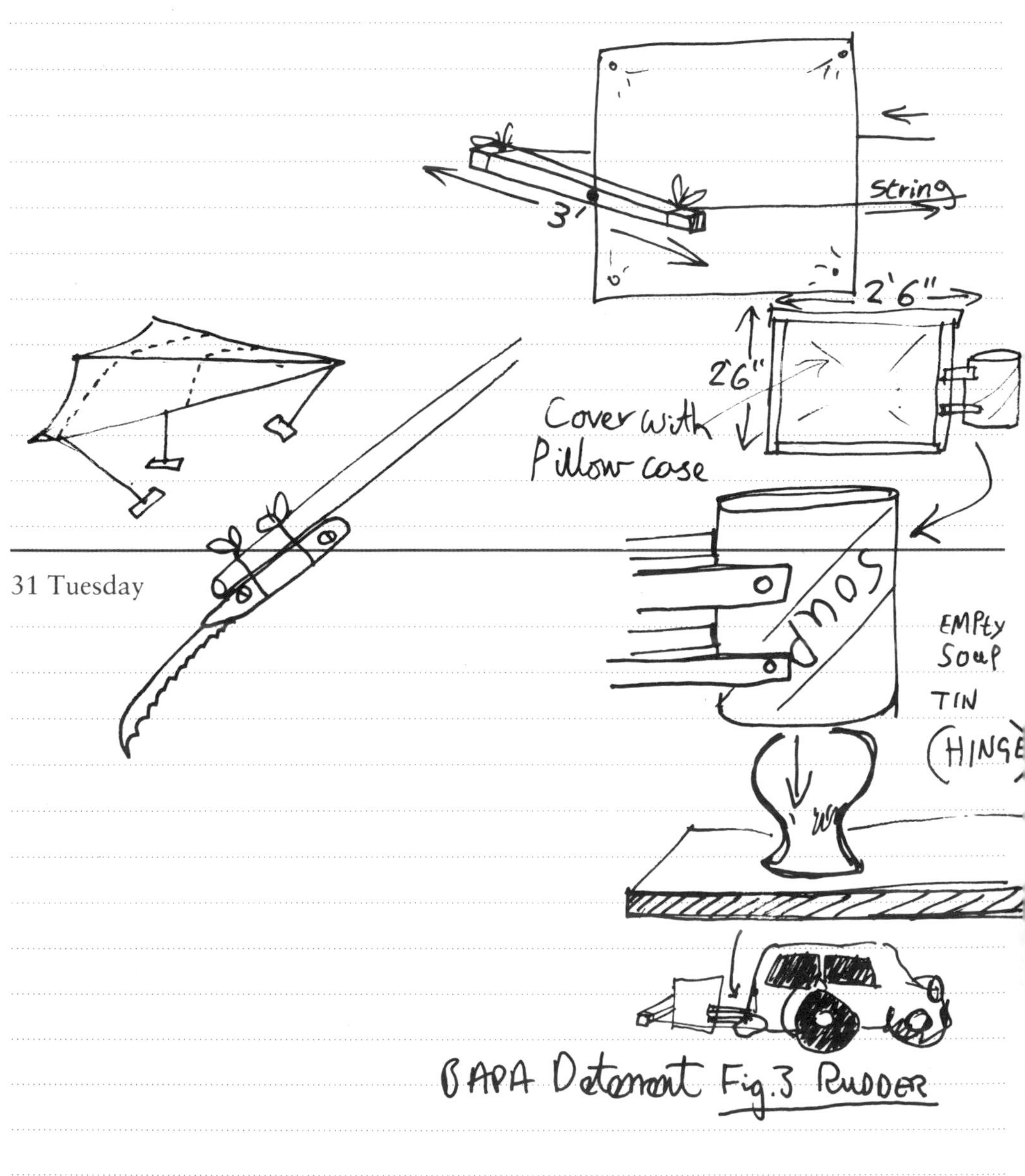

September

CRA

1 Wednesday

MRS. WICKET IN BRIGHTON

10.00 Clear Drive
10.30 DELIVERY OF HORSE POOP

2 Thursday

Morning: Fill Duvet Cover with horse poop.

Recipe Idea: RABBIT STEW
2 Pts. Hot Water
1 Rabbit
1 Plate
1 Knife
1 Fork

Boil, Serve, Eat.

September

3 Friday

Shops: More screws
Bigger screws

N.B. Need to change Traffic Light sequence, junction of Arbor Road + New Road
Requirements: Screwdriver
Pliers
Mini
Brain on
full Alert

4 Saturday

Saturday Night's the night for fighting.
(Stay in)

5 Sunday

ARBOR ROAD
NEW RD.
CONTROL BOX
- - - - - = ESCAPE ROUTE

Fig 4 Stealth Lights Plan

September

6 Monday

2–6pm Saw!
Saw!
Saw!

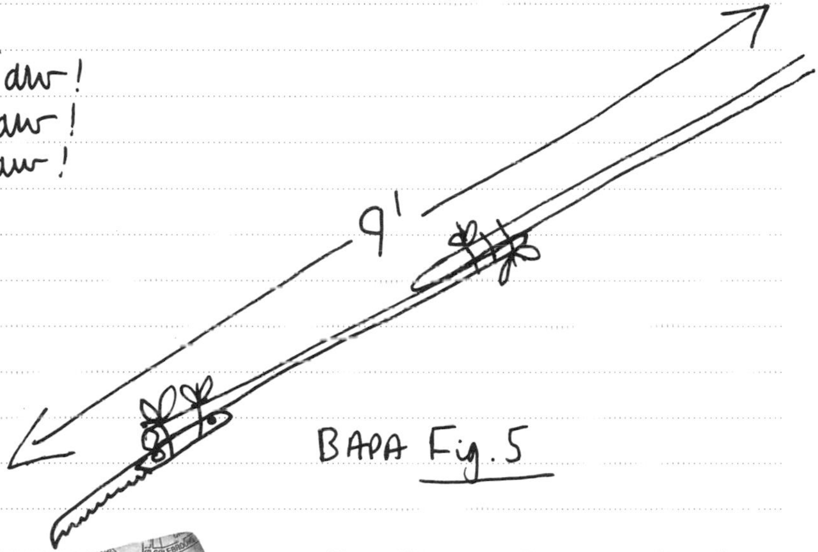

9'

BAPA Fig. 5

7 T

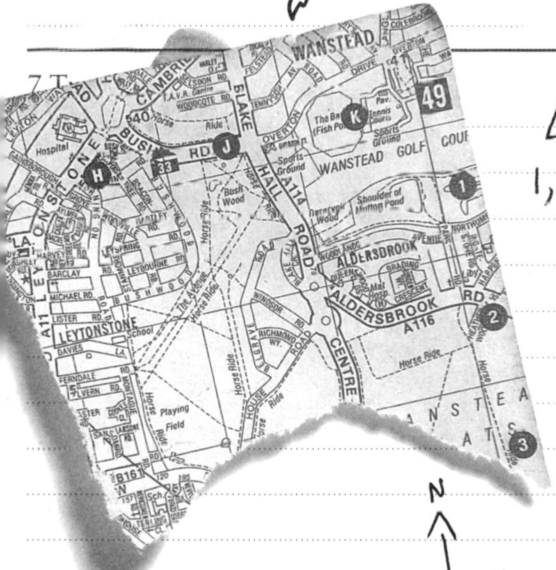

WANSTEAD
BLAKE HALL ROAD
WANSTEAD GOLF
ALDERSBROOK
LEYTONSTONE
CENTRE
Horse Ride
Playing Field

Lift
1,500 lbs
25 knots
Forward Speed

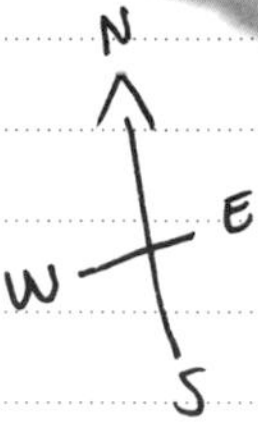

N
E
W
S

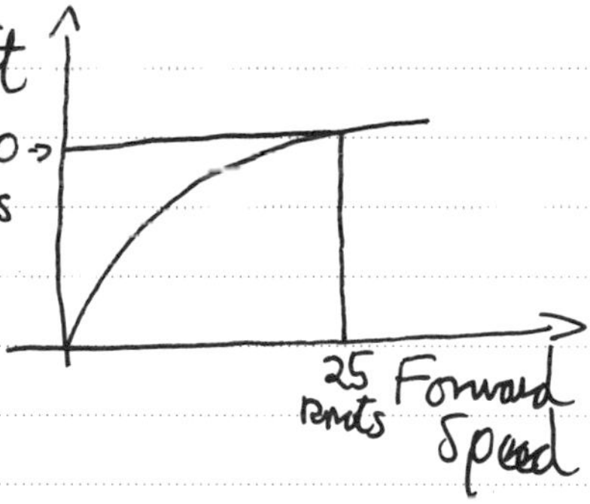

Looking Good for Mon 13th

September

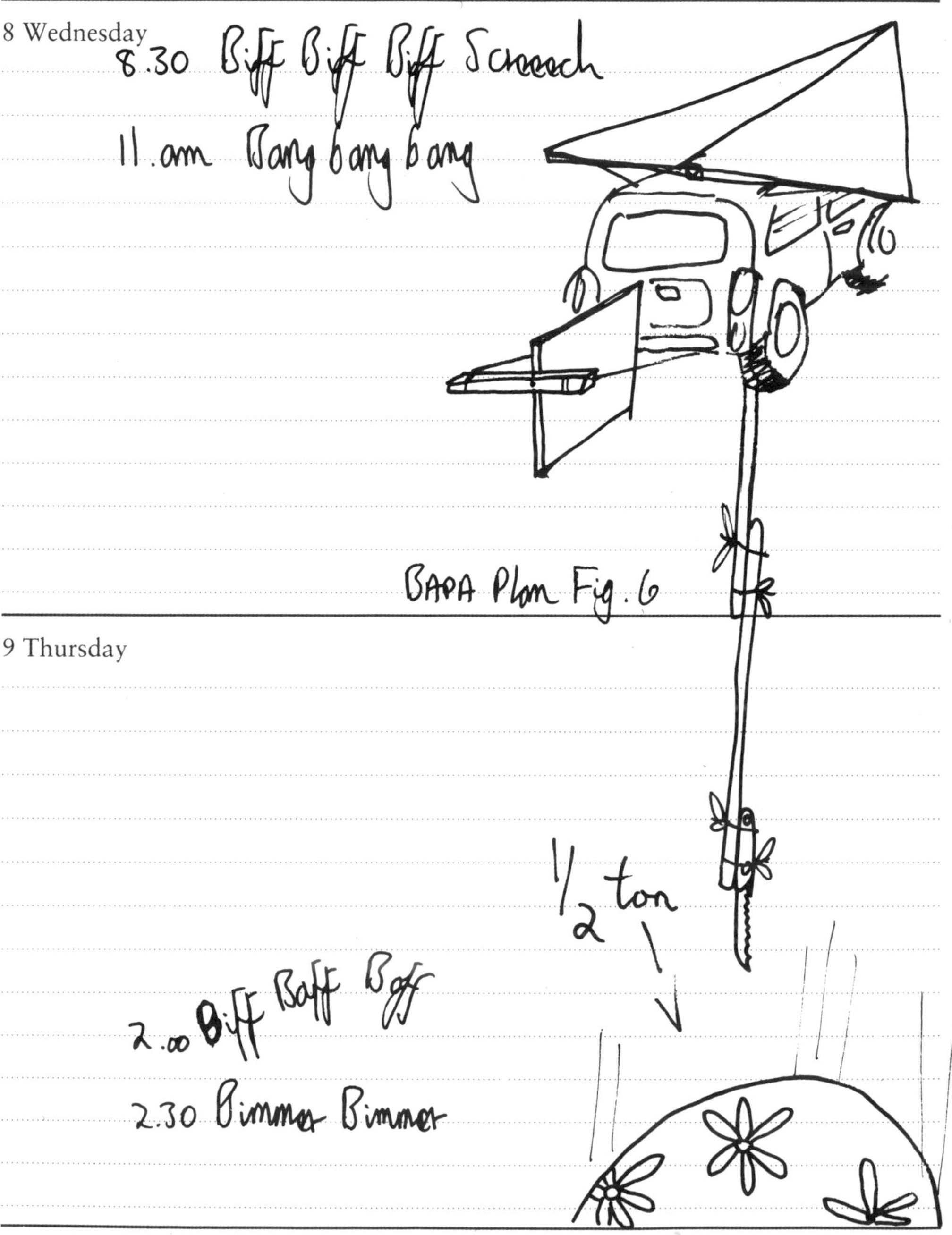
8 Wednesday
8.30 Biff Biff Biff Screeech
11.am Bang bang bang
BAPA Plan Fig. 6
9 Thursday
1/2 ton
2.00 Biff Baff Boff
2.30 Bimmer Bimmer

September

10 Friday

Nº3.

Mr Bean,
I have not slept for three nights. If the banging does not stop I will call the police.
Marvin Nº3.
(down hall.)

Oh, go away and sit on a cabbage (for the rest of your life)

11 Saturday

Dear God
Oh Lord, who giveth and taketh away. Giveth me luck on Monday but taketh me not away; unless I do something really awful like forget to flush the toilet
Yours sincerely

Mr. Bean

P.S. I hope you are well. I am fine.

12 Sunday

11.15 Church (Pray, pray, pray)

September

13 Monday

14 Tuesday

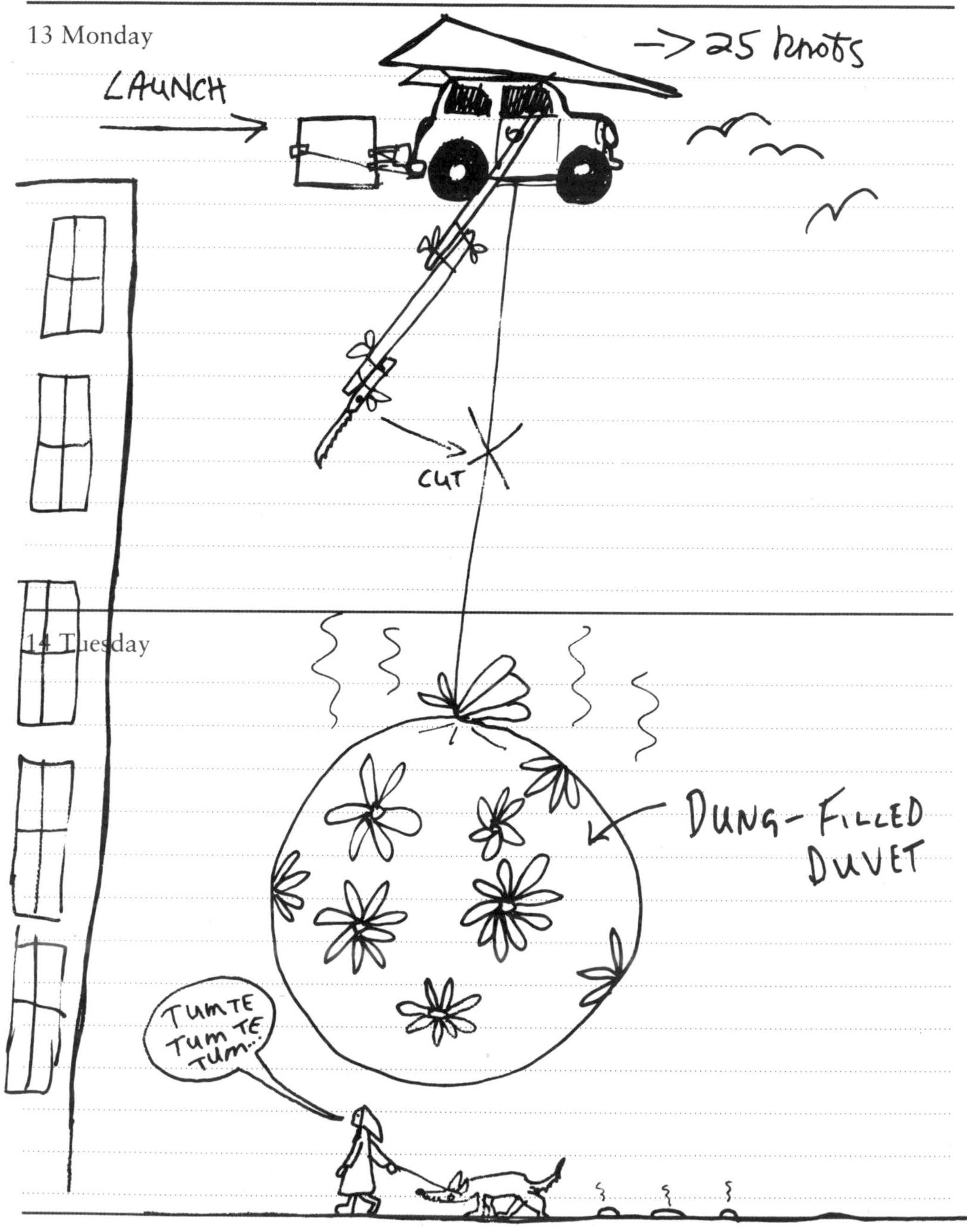

15 Wednesday

Highbury Herald September 15 1993

Bizarre man foiled

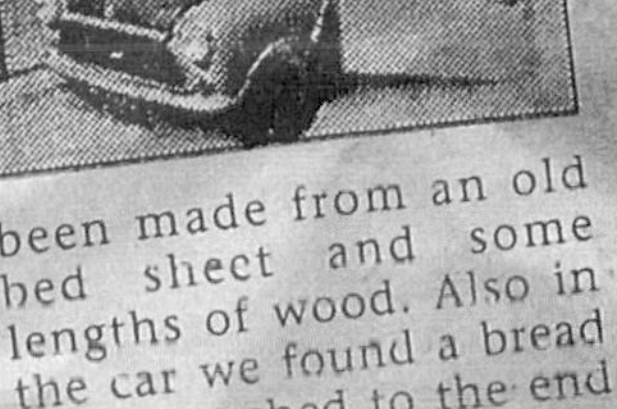

A HIGHBURY man's attempt to "put the world to rights" was foiled after police received a tip-off that a lime green mini was about to be launched from the roof of WH Smith in New Road.

The owner of the car, a Mr Bean of Arbor Road, Highbury, was first spotted by pedestrians on the street below, who alerted the police.

"The vehicle in question was fitted with a home-made set of wings, rather like a hang-glider, on the roof," said a police spokesman. "The wings upon inspection seem to have been made from an old bed sheet and some lengths of wood. Also in the car we found a bread knife attached to the end of a broom handle, and an electric fan."

Police are puzzled as Bean's possession of ton of horse

Nagging thought (re. my origins)

4.45 Police Station

11.00 Further questioning.

September

17 Friday

Classifieds

METROPLOLITAN POLICE

DUNG
FOR SALE
(HORSE)
85p/5lb bag.
All proceeds to Police
Benevolent Fund
Reply box 77.

Large collection of inse
all in sil ... sewoo
presen

LIE LOW

18 Saturday

LIE LOW

19 Sunday

LIE LOWER

September

N°3.

Dear Mr Bean,
I don't believe your car was stolen at all. I saw the horse dung on the drive, and I think you are completely mad.

Man in N°3.
(down hall)

I've a funny feeling my birthday was last Wednesday.

21 Tuesday

3.

STINK

September

22 Wednesday

NAME Mr. D. Wilkinson
ADDRESS 23A Cherry Lane
London
N5
I think your idea is great. Signed.
D. Wilkinson

YIPPEE!!

23 Thursday

9.15 Ring Mr. Wilkinson

4.30 Mr. Wilkinson for tea

Shops: Crumpets
Crusty buns
Juicy Cake
Big cake
Small cake
Stodgy cake
Lovely cake
+ other cake

September

24 Friday

20 mins

NEW IMPROVED "SNAIL" RULER

© Mr. Bean

3.00 BANK - get £500 for Mr. Wilkinson

25 Saturday

10.00 Drive Mr. Wilkinson to shops

3.15 Mr. Wilkinson's ointment

26 Sunday

10.00 Polish Mr. Wilkinson's knobs + knockers

Mr. Wilkinson borrowing car this afternoon.

10.00 Car due back

September

27 Monday

WHERE IS MR. WILKINSON?

DAM STAB
CUSS WRETCH
DISMEMBER
DISEMBOWEL

3.45 Police

WHERE OH WHERE IS MY LOVELY CAR

28 Tuesday

8.40 Catch bus to shops

9.20 Bus

4.30 Smelly bus home again

September

29 Wednesday

Poem: MIND YOUR GRANNY

If there's one thing that's not fetching
It's the sight of someone retching
So at Grandma's please do be extremely careful
If you need to vomit after tea
Then in the toilet you should be
So as not to give your Gran a sticky earful.

Mr. Bean 29 Sept 1993

7.30 Poetry Class

30 Thursday

Possible chorus: Pewky pewky retch retch
Head inside the bowl
Keeping it from Granny
Should be your intended goal.
Tra la

Show to Ms. Rosemary Hosebury

October

1 Friday

WHERE is my £500?

WHERE is my car?

WHERE is slimy puss-y slimebag Mr. Wilkinson?

London Transport
PHOTOCARD

Name of holder
MR/M S
Mr. Bean

Valid for use only by person shown with a ticket bearing the same number.

T 5328

2 Saturday

I HATE THE BUSSSS

October

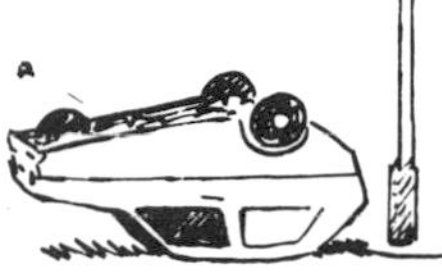

4 Monday

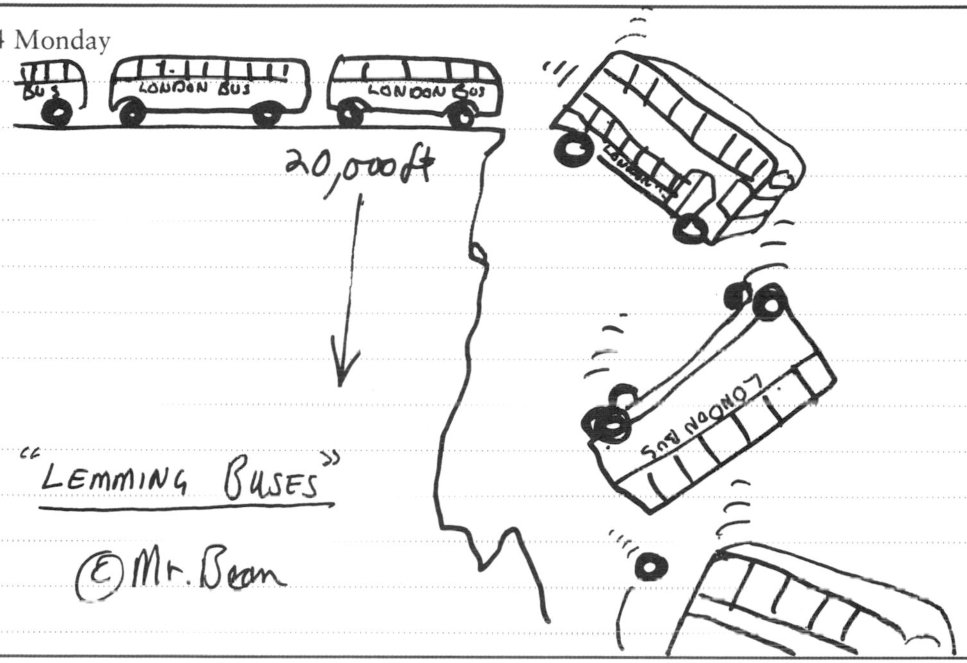

BUS
LONDON BUS
LONDON BUS
20,000 ft
"LEMMING BUSES"
© Mr. Bean

5 Tuesday

Plan: 10.00 Catch bus
10.15 Torture bus
11.00 Kill bus

RIP
LONDON BUS

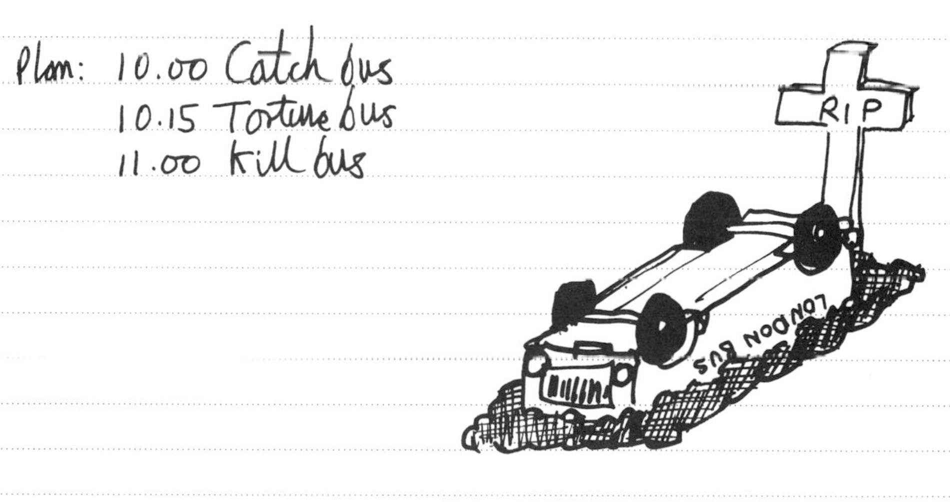

October

6 Wednesday

Shops: Acce
Celery

7.00 Start Bell Ringing

7 Thursday

That revolting couple ITV (Morning)

9.30 Bell Ringing

October

8 Friday

1.45 am Bell Ringing

9 Saturday

11.00 More Bell ringing

N°3.
Dear Mr Bean,
Some idiot
keeps ringing
my doorbell
then running
away.
Is it you?

Man in N°3
(down hall).

Heh heh
heh heh
heh!

October

11 Monday

Highbury District Council (Adult Ed. Dept.)
Council Offices
Highbury, London N10

Dear Mr Bean

I am writing on what I know is a very sensitive subject, but I hope you will appreciate my honesty and frankness.

You have been a most enthusiastic pupil at my poetry class, never failing to do your homework and always handing in on time the work which I have requested. I am afraid that I have to tell you, however, that there is something about your work which is really quite shocking, not only to myself, but also to your classmates. They are forced to bear witness to your poetry, as you always insist on reading it out loud during the class, banging the lid of your desk enthusiastically as you do so. As I cannot emphasise enough, we have nothing but admiration for your enthusiasm. But we have had complaints. You may remember that Ann Warburton was physically sick during your stirring rendition of your poem on the same subject (Vomiting), and has never returned. Dear old Derek didn't sleep for a week after the blood-letting trilogy. The class is now half the size it was at the beginning of term, and I'm sorry to say that you and your poetry are the chief cause of the decline in numbers.

12 Tuesday

Might we interest you in another subject? The Adult Education Institute has over a hundred courses running in the '93-'94 academic year and I am sure we could find one more attuned to your inclinations and enthusiasm. Car maintenance? Italian? I'm sure we could find you something. If you choose to leave our poetry class, we would naturally refund your course fee in full, and also pay the new course's fees for a full five years.

Yours sincerely

Rosemary Hosebury

Rosemary Hosebury (Ms)

Yah boo hiss

I'm Mr. Dam Bean
Not Mr. Has Bean

As you might have guessed
You've made me depressed,

10.15. Buy bottle of alcohol in shop

October

13 Wednesday

I can do rhymes
Time after Time (s)

Whiskey is lovely
es

French Foriegn Legion
010 33 43920047

Bla Blabla

~~7.30 Poetry Class~~

TEA
-CHERS

14 Thursday

Shirley where are you
Shirley Jo understand

Ring Irma

Gobble
Gobble
Gobble

More

Wicky

October

15 Friday

Do everything extremely quietly don't make any noise at all I think this might be what they call a hangover I've read about it in books move very slowly and speak very very softly do not go out close curtains sssssssssshhhhsssssssssshhhsssssssshhh

16 Saturday

9.30 Go out quietly
Shopping: Bread
Ear plugs

12.00 Come in so, so quietly
Tiptoe upstairs

Ssssshhh

17 Sunday

11.15 Don't go to church

October

18 Monday

4.15 Lemon

19 Tuesday

8.40 CAR RETURNED
YIPPEE!

God bless the Highland Police
Who returned my car
With its Reyssse (still in it)

2.10 Put music system in car
(needs new stylus)

Records for car: The Very Best of Shirley Bassey
Shirley at her Best
Best of Bassey
Bassey's Best of the Bestest

October

20 Wednesday

MICK'S KENDO CLUB
School Hall, 8.15
Wednesday Evening

Shops: Broom Handles
White sheet

~~7.30 Poetry Class~~
8.15 Kendo Class

21 Thursday

Motor Show - Earl's Court

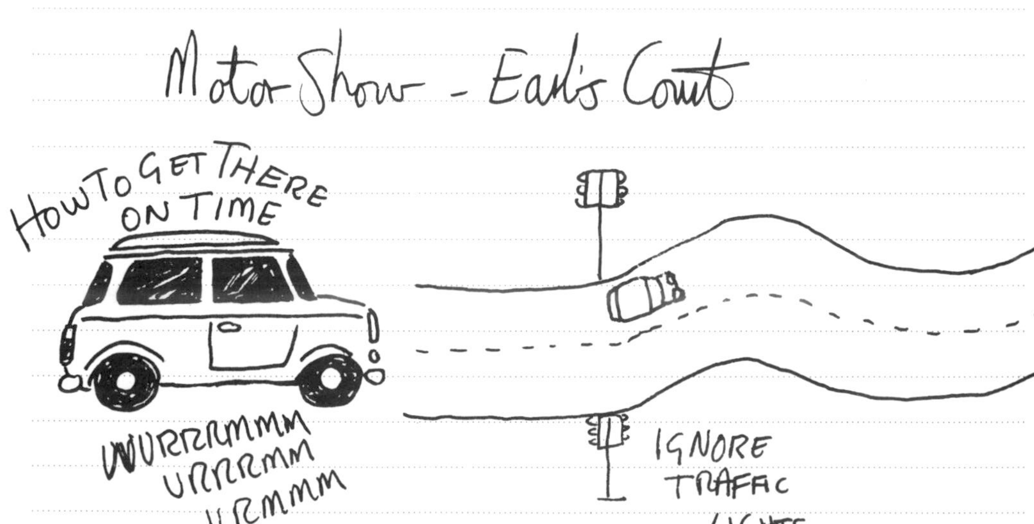

October

22 Friday

110 MPH SAFE

SCREECH!

BEEP BEEP

APPROACH PEDESTRIAN CROSSING:
1. HORN
2. ACCELERATE
3. CLOSE EYES

SQUEAL!

23 Saturday

24 Sunday

CHILDREN'S PLAYGROUND

HUMP BACKED BRIDGE

PEDESTRIAN PRECINCT

TRAFFIC JAM (TAKE SHORT CUT)

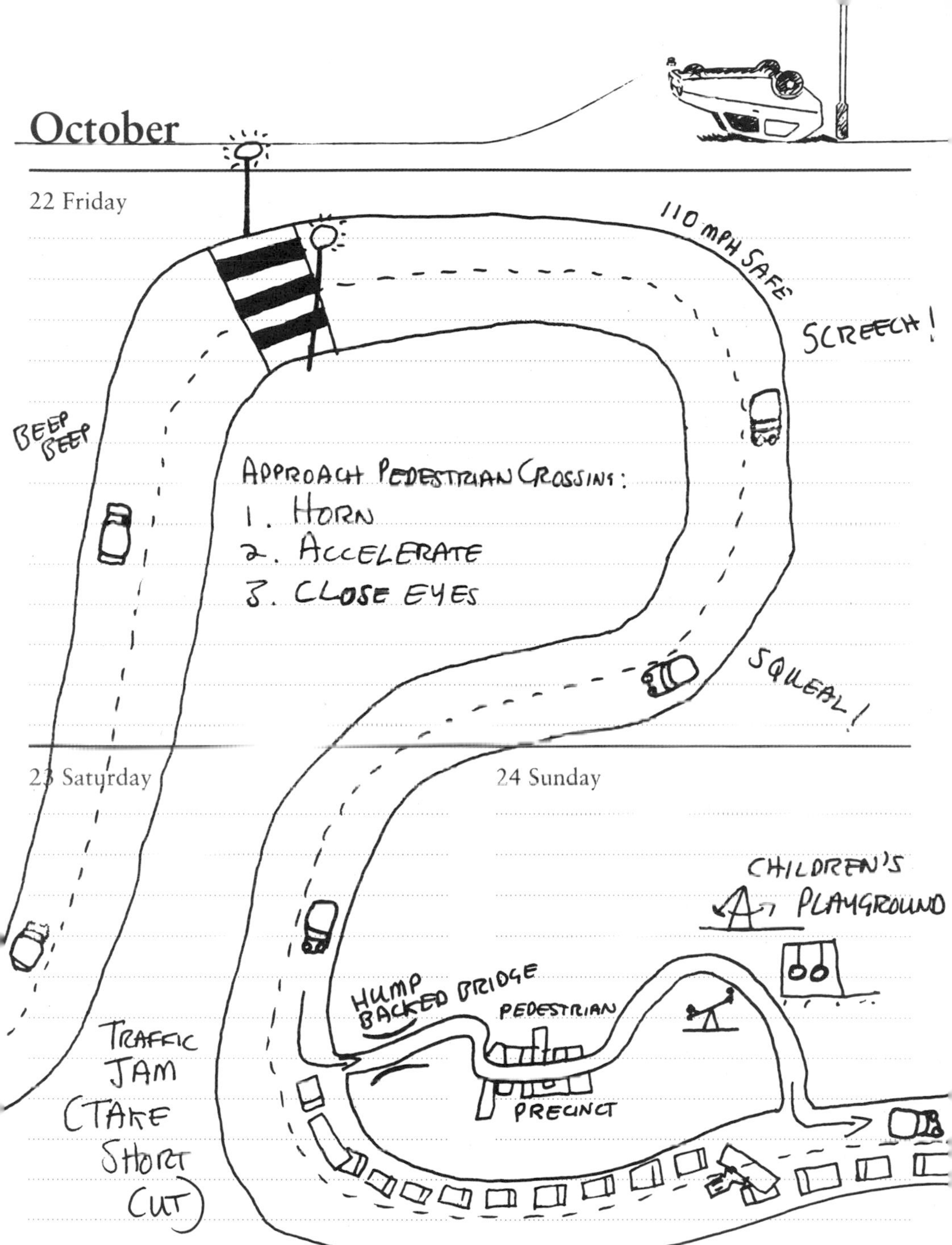

October

25 Monday

Petrol
Lettuce
Stamps

I thought girls
Always had curls

HAY
STACK →

85 MPH SAFE

26 Tuesday

WET ROAD:
1. ACCELERATE
2. SWERVE FROM
SIDE TO SIDE

ROUNDABOUT:
GO ROUND 3 TIMES
FLAT OUT

October

27 Wednesday

WARP SPEED

ROAD NARROWS

RELIANT ROBIN

POLICE CAR

NA NUR NA NUR!

OUT

8.15 Kendo Class

28 Thursday

Plan: ~~8.15 Go to Japan~~

~~12.30 Have lunch~~

~~4.00 Comehome~~

Notpossible

October

29 Friday

30 Saturday

31 Sunday

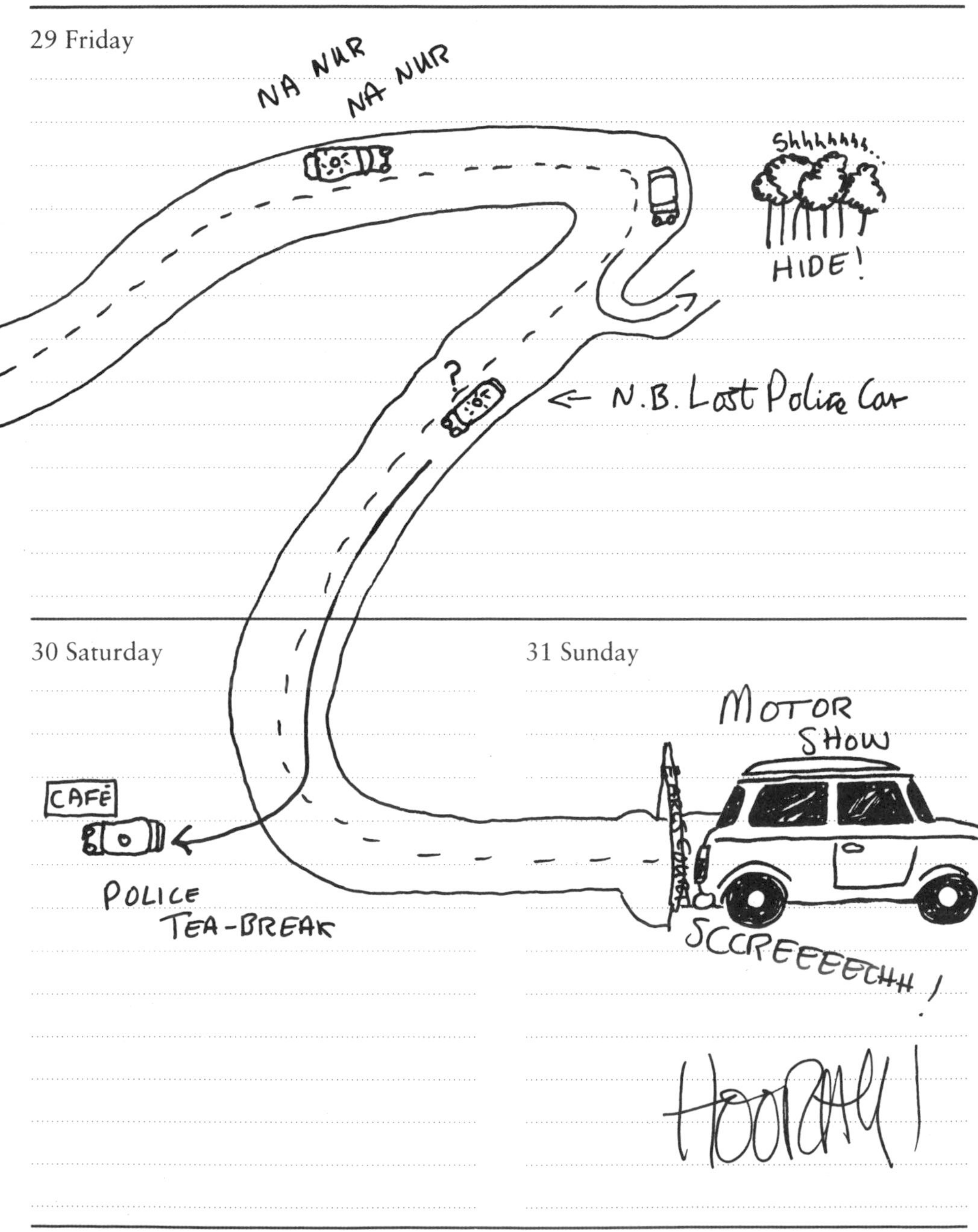

November

1 Monday

Oven broken – Ring Gas Man

Buy salad stuff : Tomatoes
Cucumber
Weeds
Insects
Soil

Dinner: Salad & Bread

2 Tuesday

9.00 Gas Man

12.00 Oven still broken

Lunch: Salad

stupid STUPID Gas Man

Dinner: Salad

November

3 Wednesday

8.15: Try and cook without oven (Lamb chops)

9.00: FIRE BRIGADE

2.45am Sleep.

4 Thursday

9.00 Shops: Flour x 30lbs
Eggs

Plot plot plot plot plot

November

5 Friday → Guy Fawkes Night

Flipping angerous (flipper!)

plot plot plot plot plot

plot treason plot treason plot treason treason plot

8pm. Bonfire Party (in Park)

GET THEM WITH FLOUR BOMB
(then throw eggs) if time

6 Saturday

9.00 Police station
Questioning

all day

7 Sunday

Fireworks Fright

POLICE WERE CALLED to a bonfire party last night where a man was apprehended under suspicion of intending to plant a large explosive on the bonfire.

"What we suspected of being a large bomb turned out to be a bag of flour and eggs", said event organiser Don Haze. "When I dragged him out of the tree he told me he was just about to make a cake."

Mr Bean, of Arbor Road, London, was detained ...

November

8 Monday

ALL THE SMOKERS IN THE WORLD

VROOM! VROOM!

"COMMON SENSE"

© Mr. Bean

9 Tuesday

1.00 Egg

7.00 Another egg

METROPOLITAN POLICE
RECEIPT

your ref:

our ref:

Surrendered Goods

2 BROOM HANDLES

P.C. R. Leans

The above items have been confiscated pending a decision by local magistrates

8.15
Micks Kendo Club

Challenge Mick to DUEL

5.15 Duel at Dawn

Requirements : Broom handle
Sheet

Report : 4.45 Hospital (re. neck brace)
6.00 Police (re. broom handles)

November

12 Friday

Engagements/Marr

GOBB – GUMMER
The engagement is announced between Irma Edith Gobb, librarian, and Giles Gummer, anaesthetist.

PACE – PARKES
The engagement is announced between Carina Pace, video producer, and Roger Parkes, sculptor/cordon bleu ch...

WHAT!?!

4.15 Stake out

13 Saturday

14 Sunday

Plan

LIBRARY

PARK

AMBUSH

HIT! HIT! HIT!

BEAN WITH BIG STICK

BUSH

GET AWAY

MINI

Usual route of G. Gummer

November

15 Monday

SHIRLEY BASSEY LETTER

v. v. v. v. v. v. v. v. v. v. v. v. important

4.10 Post Box

16 Tuesday

If I was going to choose a day
I would choose Choose-day.

~~4.07 Gummer Ambush~~ POLICE SUSPICIOUS

HIDE DIARY

GUMMER

STRETCH

TUG

November

17 Wednesday

HIDE DIARY

12.15 POLICE CALLING ROUND.

~~8.15 Mick's Kendo Club~~

N.B. COUNTRY DANCING next Monday

18 Thursday

TOAST RECIPE

Burn Bread
Eat

November

19 Friday

Shirley Bassey
Entertainments

Las Vegas • Hollywood • Monte Carlo • London

Mr Bean
c/o Mrs Wickets
"Daffodils"
Room 2
12 Arbor Road
London N10

Dear Mr Bean

Thank you for your recent letter to Ms Bassey: I'm sorry I've been so late in replying.

I am sorry to say that the vocal microphones used by Ms Bassey during her performances are extremely expensive items, and it would be impossible to send them as souvenirs to fans who request them.

Enclosed is a signed photograph as partial compensation!

Yours sincerely

Richard Kershaw

Richard Kershaw
Technical Manager
Shirley Bassey Ents.

Write again

November

22 Monday

START →

1 – 2 Tum TeeTum Tra la la

7.00 Country Dancing

23 Tuesday

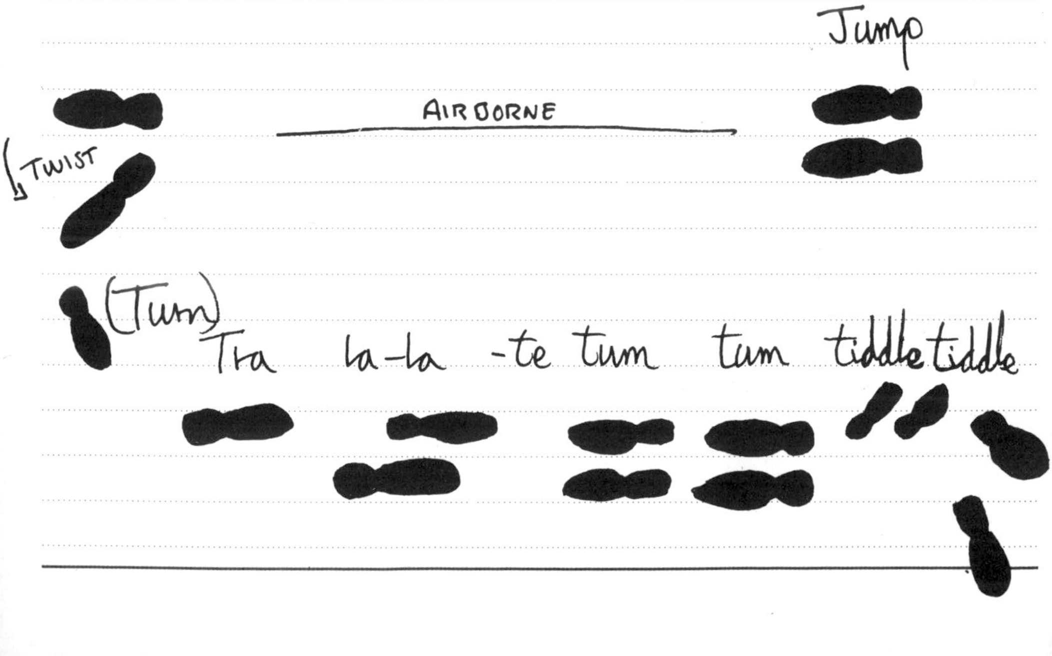

Jump

AIRBORNE

TWIST

(Turn)

Tra la-la -te tum tum tiddle tiddle

November

24 Wednesday

Boff Boff

Dum

Bang
Bang

Trrrrrummm

Titty

Deedee
Deedee
Dee

Voopp!

25 Thursday

Hop

La -la -la

Skip

teedly - dee Bink Bink Boodle Baff

FINISH

November

26 Friday

2.00
Shoes
Honey

27 Saturday

Shirley Bassey
Entertainments

Las Vegas • Hollywood • Monte Carlo • London

Mr Bean
c/o Mrs Wickets
"Daffodils"
Room 2
12 Arbor Road
London N10

Dear Mr Bean

I acknowledge receipt of your letter of the 17th of July.

I understand that we misread the request in your last letter, and that there was no grammatical error. Your request was to BE one of Ms Bassey's microphones, rather than to posses one.

I should warn you that, in accordance with the policy of this office, your letter has been passed to the police.

Yours sincerely

Adrian Silverman

Adrian Silverman
for Shirley Bassey Ents.

November

29 Monday Mrs. Wicket going to Bournemouth

Look after Kipper

KIPPER

Please look after Kipper. He is very sensitive and needs feeding every day
Mrs Wicket

7.00 Country Dancing

Tra-la-la-dee-dum-te-tum

1-2 1-2 1-2 1-2 and rest.

25 days to Christmas

December

1 Wednesday

N° 3.

Dear Mr Bean,
Have you heard
that barking from
Mrs Wicket's?

Man in N° 3.
(down hall).

It is you that's
barking!

Nagging thought

2 Thursday

Nagging thought

December

3 Friday

Nagging thought

4 Saturday

8.00 Nagging tho

oh my God NO

AAAARGHH

12 MIDNIGHT: Put Kipper's corpse in middle of road (Act natural)

5 Sunday

MRS. WICKET BACK FROM BOURNEMOUTH

Dear ~~Mrs~~ Mrs. Wicket

I was so sorry to hear that Kipper had escaped and been run over while my back was turned. I think I was ironing at the time, ~~but~~ although I did hear brakes and, thinking it was a bat screeching sub-sonically, ~~I~~

December

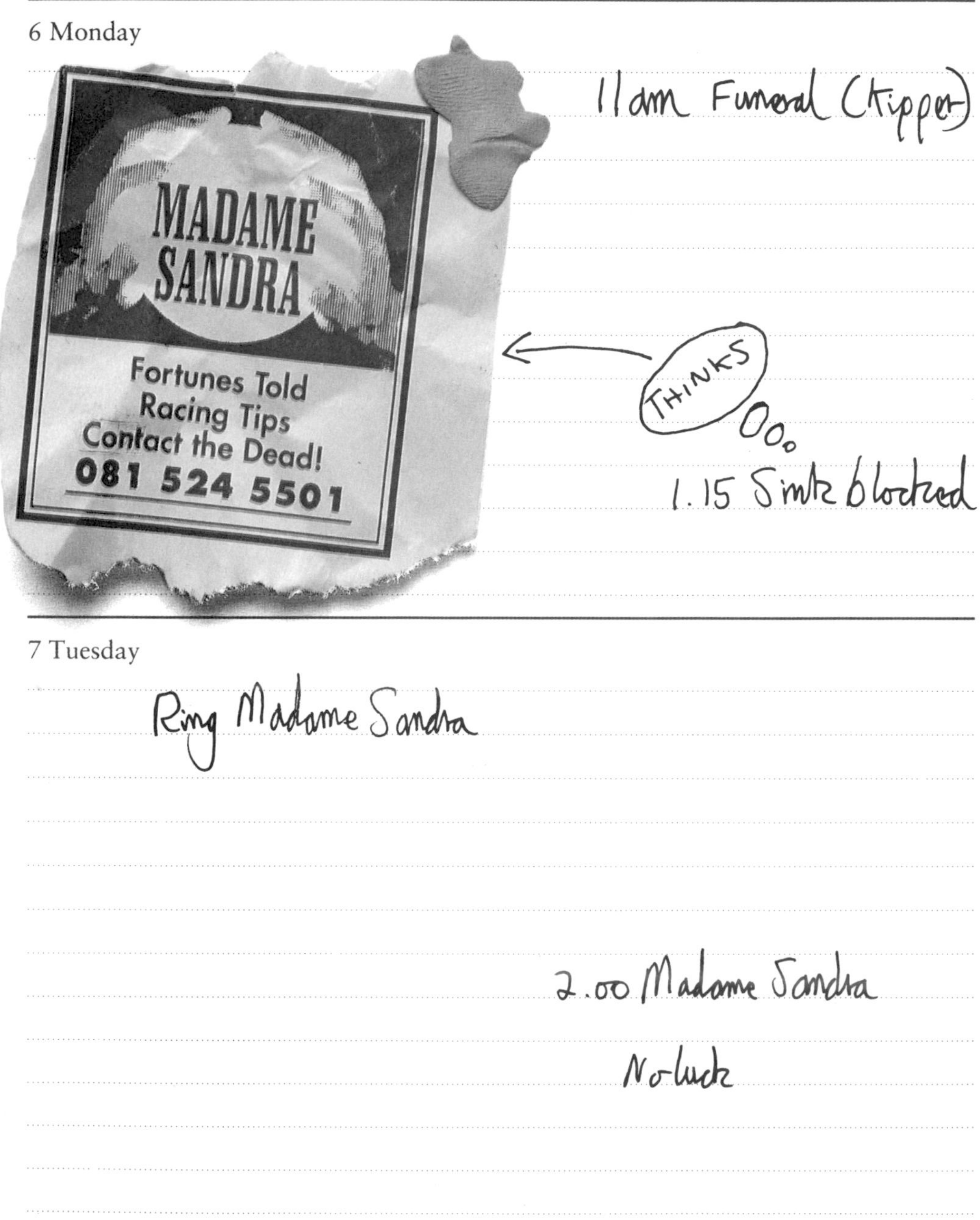
6 Monday
MADAME SANDRA
Fortunes Told
Racing Tips
Contact the Dead!
081 524 5501
11am Funeral (Kipper)
THINKS
1.15 Sink blocked
7 Tuesday
Ring Madame Sandra
2.00 Madame Sandra
No luck

December

8 Wednesday

11.00 Madame Sandra
(Some progress)

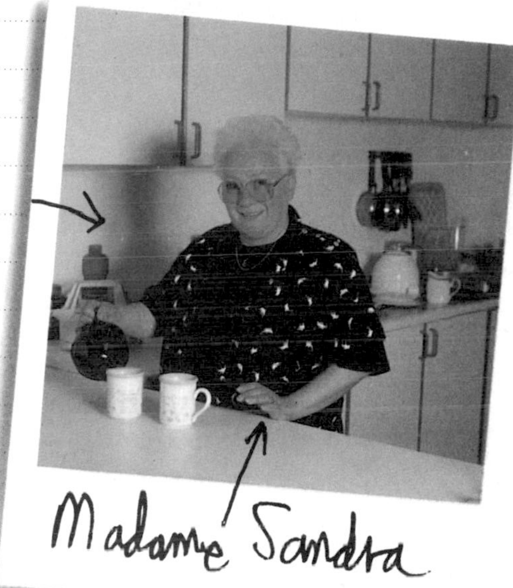

9 Thursday

11.45 Madame Sandra

MADE CONTACT WITH MUM

Question: Where is the plunger for the sink?

Answer: Under the stairs

12.10 Unblock sink ✓

ALLINONE STUMPS
© Mr. Bean

December

10 Friday

1.00 Crisps

11 Saturday

2 weeks till Chrizzy

12 Sunday

December

13 Monday

9.15 Madame Sandra
(Talk to Charles Dickens)

Q: What was supposed to happen to Edwin Drood?

A: Hadn't made up his mind.

14 Tuesday

Dear ~~Santa~~ Mr. Claus ← more respectful

I hope you are well. I am fine.

There really is not very long to go now until Christmas, so I thought I might write ~~and~~ with a provisional list of presents in order of preference:

1. A quantity of High Explosive (Semtex, or equivalent)
2. Small rubber fork.
3. New mother
4. Brass hook (Toilet door)
5. t.b.a.

December

15 Wednesday

10.00 Buy New TV

+ Radio Times
TV Times
~~Financial Times~~
TV Quick

QUICK!

16 Thursday

NEW ROOM PLANS FOR CHRISTMAS

(TO ACCOMODATE TV)

DOOR

WINDOW

TV

BED

WINDOW

CHAIR

December

17 Friday

18 Saturday

19 Sunday

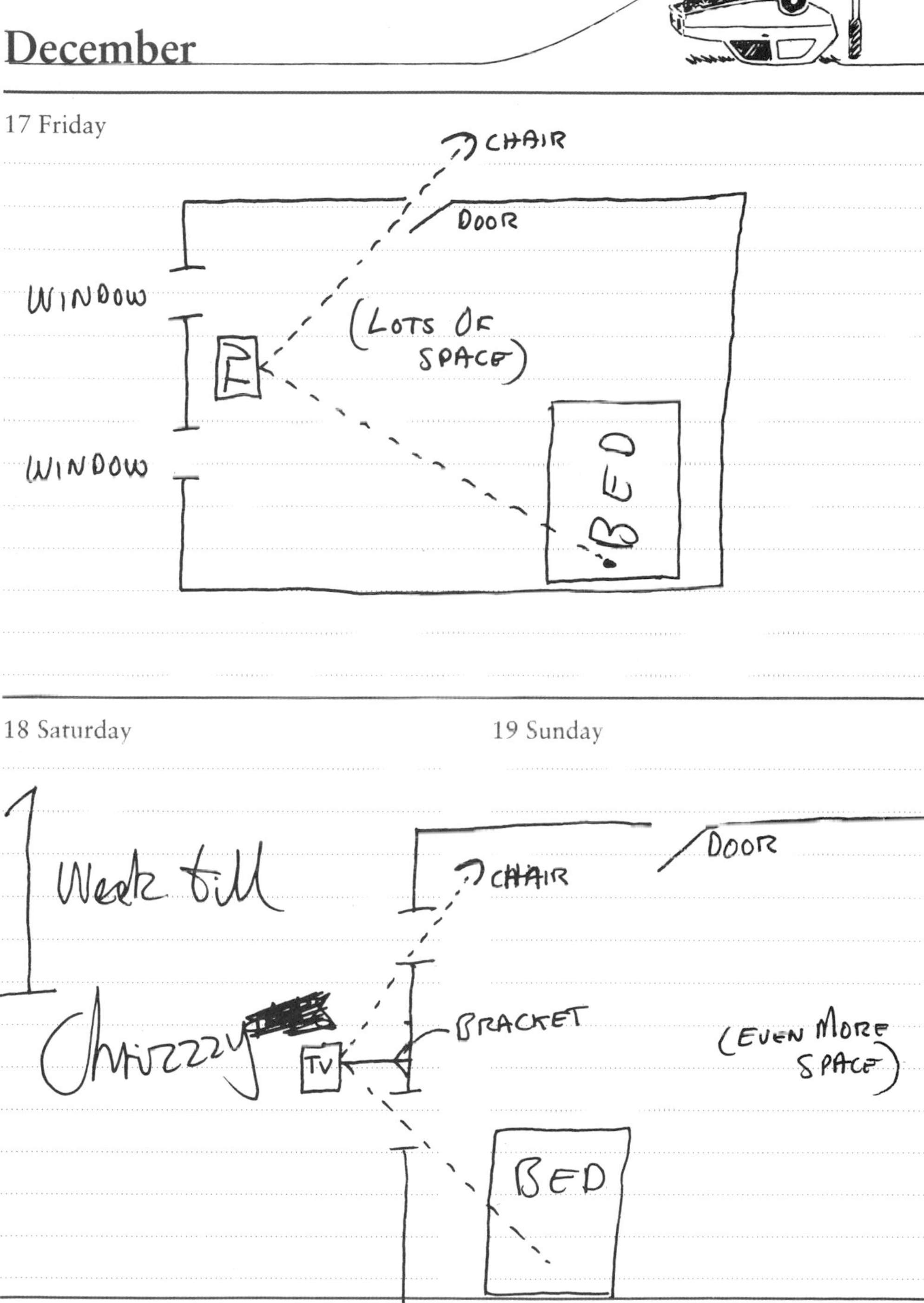

December

20 Monday

BED

DOOR

WINDOW

CHAIR

(MOST SPACE)

TV

21 Tuesday

("Daffodils")

Dear Mr. Claus

I hope you are well. I am fine. Only four days till the birthday of our Lord Jesus Christ, and I've had a change of heart: I would now like a Drum Kit which I can bash and bash and bash

New order

1. Snare drum
2. Cymbal
3. Bass drum
4. Tom-Tom
4a. Hi-hat
5. Tom-Tom
6. " "
7. " "
8. Brass hook (TOILET DOOR)
9.

22. Semtex

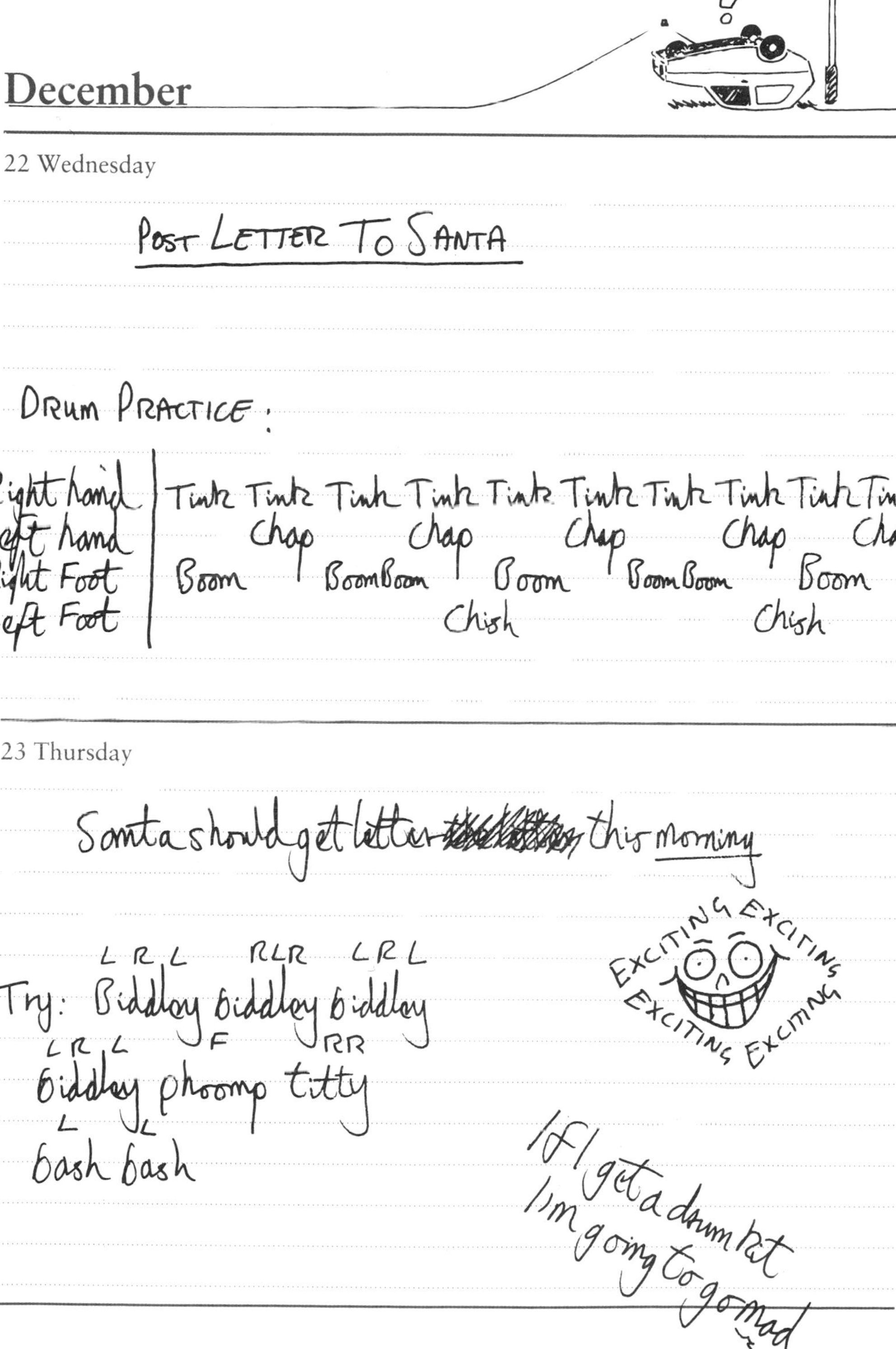
December
?
22 Wednesday
POST LETTER TO SANTA
DRUM PRACTICE:
Right hand | Tink Tink Tink Tink Tink Tink Tink Tink Tink Tink
Left hand | Chap Chap Chap Chap Chap
Right Foot | Boom BoomBoom Boom BoomBoom Boom
Left Foot | Chish Chish
23 Thursday
Santa should get letter this morning
EXCITING EXCITING EXCITING EXCITING EXCITING EXCITING
LRL RLR LRL
Try: Biddley biddley biddley
LRL F RR
biddley phoomp titty
L L
bash bash
If I get a drum kit I'm going to go mad

December

24 Friday

I want a drum kit
I want a drum kit
Tiddle diddle rapple rapple
Bum Boom tish.

Shops: Buy cracker

Buy brass hook.

25 Saturday Christmas Day

OOOh! BRASS HOOK for Christmas!

Just what I NEED!!

No other presents

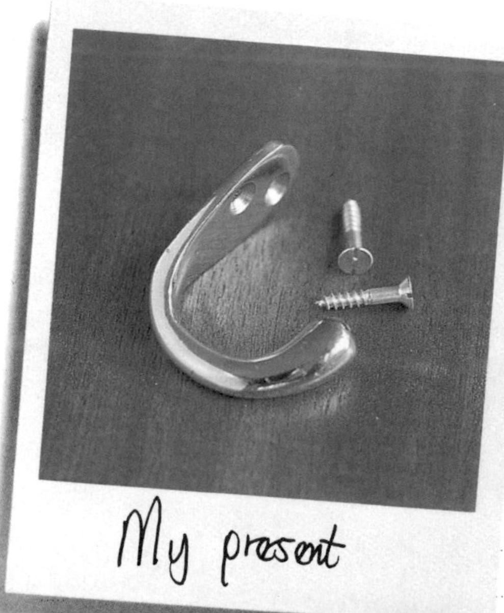

My present

(Cracker didn't crack – send back to man)

December

27 Monday   Boxing Day

10.00 Go to Park (empty)

~~Practise on drum kit~~

No shops open

Evening: stay in

28 Tuesday

Water plant (in next door garden)

~~Practise on drum kit~~

I don't like Christmas very much if I had to be honest

December

29 Wednesday

Practise on drum kit

Shops: Bread,
Hazelnut
Tangerine?

30 Thursday

9.00 Bird Watching

COMMON WADER

BACK

INFLIGHT

7.00 Common Wader
(Gas Mark 7
2-2½ hrs.)

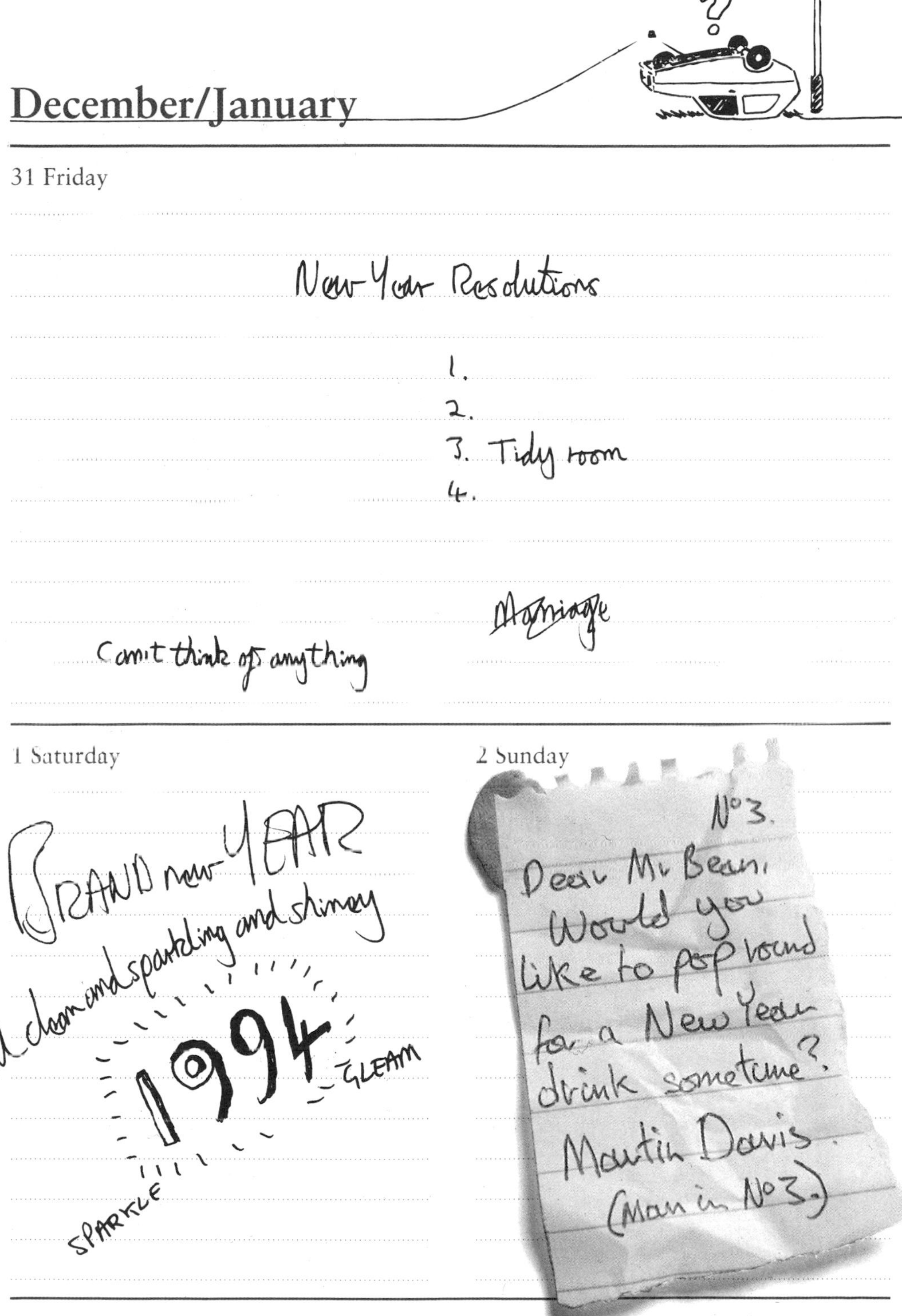

?

December/January

31 Friday

New Year Resolutions

1.
2.
3. Tidy room
4.

~~Marriage~~

Can't think of anything

1 Saturday

BRAND new YEAR
All clean and sparkling and shiney

1994

GLEAM

SPARKLE

2 Sunday

No3.
Dear Mr Bean,
Would you
like to pop round
for a New Year
drink sometime?
Martin Davis
(Man in No3.)

P.T.O →

* Bank Holiday

1994 Year Planner

	January	February	March	April	May	June
Mon						
Tue		1	1			
Wed		2	2			1
Thu		3				2
Fri		4				3
Sat	1					4
Sun	2				1	5
Mon	3*				2*	6*
Tue	4*				3	7
Wed	5				4	8
Thu	6				5	9
Fri	7				6	10
Sat	8				7	11
Sun	9				8	12
Mon	10				9	13
Tue	11				10	14
Wed	12				11	15
Thu	13				12	16
Fri	14					17
Sat	15				14	18
Sun	16				15	19
Mon	17			18	16	20
Tue	18	22		19	17	21
Wed	19	23	23	20	18	22
Thu	20	24	24	21	19	23
Fri	21	25	25	22	20	24
Sat	22	26	26	23	21	25
Sun	23	27	27	24	22	26
Mon	24	28	28	25	23	27
Tue	25		29	26	24	28
Wed	26		30	27	25	29
Thu	27		31	28	26	30
Fri	28			29	27	
Sat	29			30	28	
Sun	30				29	
Mon	31				30*	
Tue					31	
	January	February	March	April	May	June
	3 UK, R of Ireland 4 Scotland		17 Ireland (N & R)	1 UK, R of Ireland 4 England, Ireland (N & R), Wales	2 UK 30 UK	6 R of Ireland

BURY HATCHET

* Bank Holiday

1994 Year Planner

	July	August	September	October	November	December
Mon		1*				
Tue		2			1	
Wed		3			2	
Thu		4	1		3	1
Fri	1	5	2		4	2
Sat	2	6	3	1	5	3
Sun	3	7	4	2	6	4
Mon	4	8	5	3	7	5
Tue	5	9	6	4	8	6
Wed	6	10	7	5	9	7
Thu	7	11	8	6	10	8
Fri	8	12	9	7	11	9
Sat	9	13	10	8	12	10
Sun	10	14	11	9	13	11
Mon	11	15	12	10	14	12
Tue	12*	16	13	11	15	13
Wed	13	17	14	12	16	14
Thu	14	18	15	13	17	15
Fri	15	19	16	14	18	16
Sat	16	20	17 10.00 SEX	15	19	17
Sun	17	21	18 CHANGE?	16	20	18
Mon	18	22	19 (Dr. Lahote)	17	21	19
Tue	19	23	20	18	22	20
Wed	20	24	21	19	23	21
Thu	21	25	22	20	24	22
Fri	22	26	23	21	25	23
Sat	23	27	24	22	26	24
Sun	24	28	25	23	27	25
Mon	25	29*	26	24	28	26*
Tue	26	30	27	25	29	27*
Wed	27	31	28	26	30	28
Thu	28		29	27		29
Fri	29		30	28		30
Sat	30			29		31
Sun	31			30		
Mon				31*		
Tue						
	July	August	September	October	November	December
	12 N Ireland	1 R of Ireland, Scotland 29 England, N Ireland Wales		3 R of Irelland		26 UK, R of Ireland 27 UK, R of Ireland

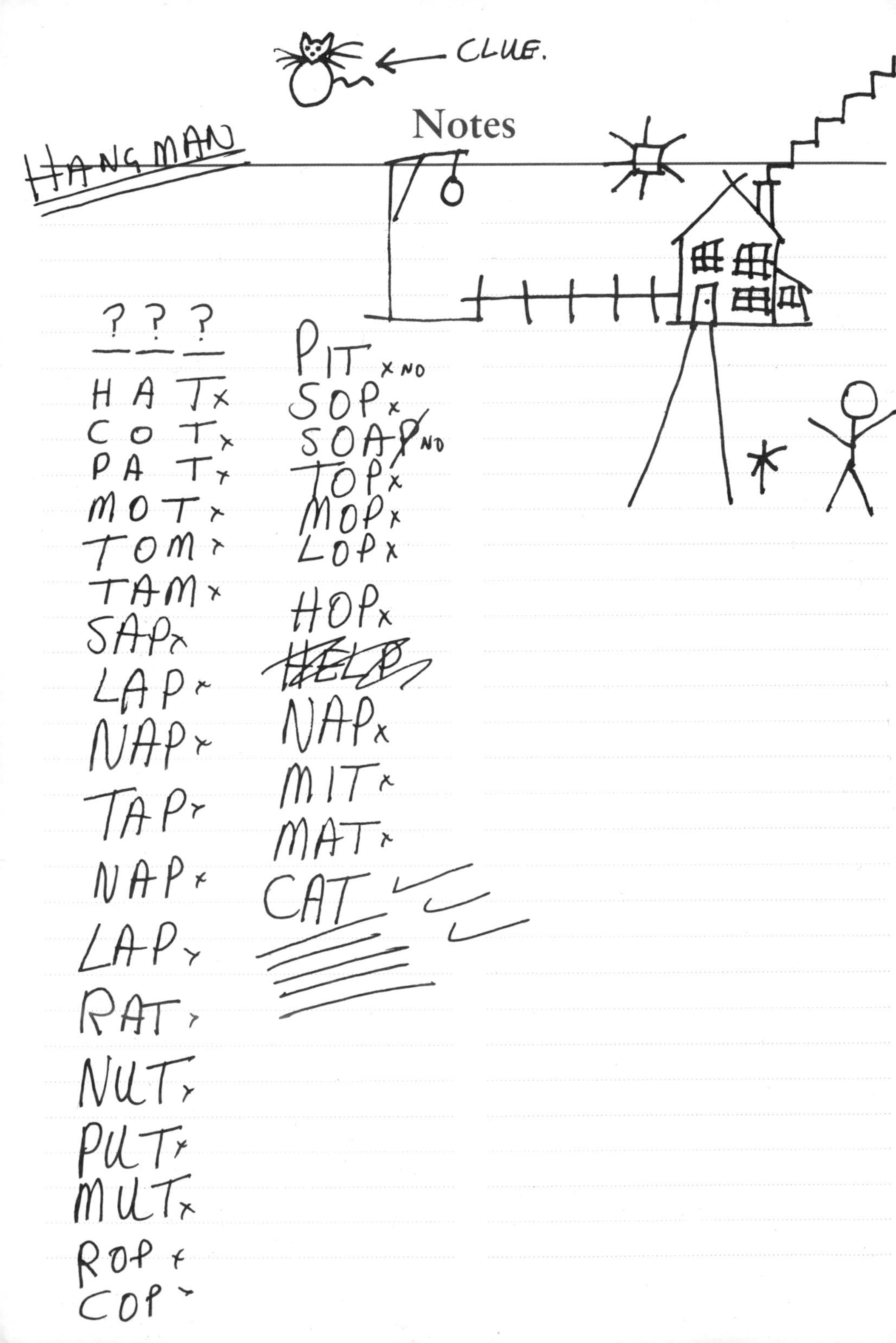
CLUE.
Notes
HANGMAN
? ? ?
HAT
COT
PAT
MOT
TOM
TAM
SAP
LAP
NAP
TAP
NAP
LAP
RAT
NUT
PUT
MUT
ROP
COP
PIT NO
SOP
SOAP NO
TOP
MOP
LOP
HOP
NAP
MIT
MAT
CAT

Chadwell School for Boys

Term: SUMMER TERM, 1971 Name: [illegible]EAN

Subject	Mark	Comments	
History	35%	He has no sense of history. But then, of course, he has no sense.	T.A.P.R.
Chemistry	53%	He is inventive. As a result, form 5B is lucky to be alive.	T.A.B.
Mathematics	94%	An obnoxious, self-satisfied, self-centred, shabby, dribbling, bone-idle, toadying cow-pat of a pupil; his most revolting quality being that he is quite, quite brilliant.	M.J.L.
Physics	65%	Very encouraging. A boy died when co-operating with his lie-detector experiment, as you know, but nevertheless the exam results are excellent.	Mr Hutt
Geography	54%	A surprisingly good result considering he only succeeded in finding the classroom twice this term	K.W.
Biology	41%	He really has no idea, but then hopefully he will never breed.	P.A.B.
Religious Knowledge	25%	No progress this year sadly. He once claimed that he worshipped the God of Lemonade which rather confused us all, I'm afraid.	N.N.
Art.	58%	He draws well, but has difficulty with nudes (looking at them).	P.B.

Good luck. He'll need it. S Love

Headmaster

£10
BANK OF ENGLAND
TEN
POUNS
£10
UNO 3662

Notes

PLAN
1. Photocopy this x 10 million
(Joan's Copy Shop
10 Slip St.)
then 2.
it.

Graph

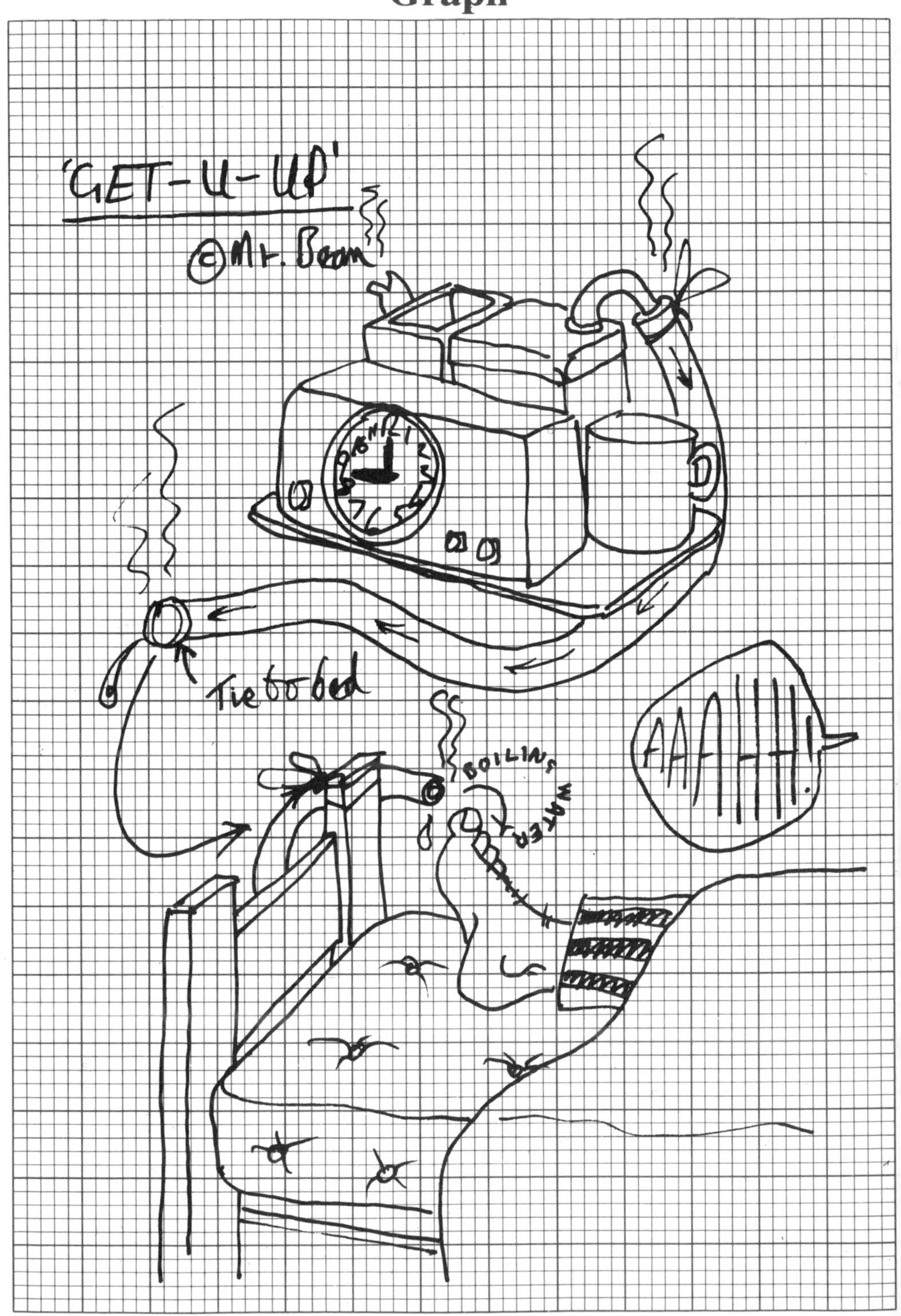

Graph

£3m. for a cup o' tea guv?

Lucky George Wilkinson, of no fixed abode, landed more than the price of a cuppa when Littlewoods coughed up a record £3,000,000 yesterday.

"I'm over the moon," he told our reporter, "Three months ago I lost my last £500 on a racehorse and have been sleeping rough ever since." George, 63, said that winning the pools will not change him except that after rubbing shoulders with some of "Britain's grubbiest" he might just start mixing with a better class of person.

he first thing I'm go